Discipline for LIFE!
- One Step at a Time

Discipline for LIFE!
- One Step at a Time

Madelyn Swift

Stairway Education
Programs

Fort Worth, Texas

Stairway Education Programs
2100 Northwest Highway, Suite 1068
Grapevine, Texas 76051

Printed in the United States of America
First printing: June, 1995

Library of Congress Cataloging-in-Publication Data
95-092132

Swift, Madelyn, 1950-
Discipline for life: one step at a time.

ISBN: 1-8807069-00-3

The paper used in this publication meets the minimum requirements of American National Standard for Information Sciences - Permanence of Paper for Printed Library Materials, ANZI Z39.48-1984

Stairway Education
Programs

To the three men in my life: John, Kris, and Tim.

Acknowledgments

So many people have influenced this book that it would be impossible to mention them all. I wish first to thank Karen Hale who could "see" this book before it was there, who could always find the look I wanted, who nourished and supported me throughout its writing, and who truly gives life to the phrase, "no hill for a stepper."

Special gratitude goes to Victoria Ryland Mathies, the editor, for her professionalism, her understanding of the material, her sense of humour, and her belief in the project.

I wish to thank my early friends, Linda, Evelyn, Sheila, Vicky, Kathy, Nancy, Susie, Norma, and Sandra who spent countless hours discussing and practicing terrific parenting and kept me from going crazy as the mother of young children. I also want to thank my later friends, Jackie, Wendy, Arlene, Gerti, Diane, Colleen, Shauna, Nancy, Francie, Carole, and Jenny, who shared stories, families, food, strengths and weaknesses.

Thank you also to David Gavin and Len Oszustowicz who gently and generously taught me about the publishing industry.

I am indebted to Shari Wells and Ann Jones, who organized my professional life so well that I was able to find time to write.

Finally, I wish to thank Kris and Tim, who taught and continue to teach me much of what I need to know and whose existence was essential to this book. I owe my greatest appreciation to JDS who believed in me and supported me in <u>every</u> way.

Foreword

Many years ago, in a small town in northern Ontario, a group of mothers got together with their toddlers and preschool age children to share a warm mug of coffee, to chat, and to watch our children learn to socialize and play. For many of us just coming together that one morning a week brought us face to face with some serious challenges: How did we get two, or three, small children dressed, snow-suited, and off to a group which we knew they would enjoy, and we needed? How did we cope with the obstructiveness of a two and a half year old who was really planning upon staying in pajamas all day and coloring houses with flowers in the yard? And what did we do about those recalcitrant little ones who once in the back seat, buckled in for safety, still had arms long enough to torment the child beside them. And what did we do with our own frustrations and angers, and often our I-don't get-enough-sleep-at-night-I'm-bone-weary spirits?

In a way the solution was in our coming together and nurturing one another. But we were lucky; we were so lucky. Firstly, we loved our children with an unconcealed passion and an irrepressible hopefulness. And most importantly, we had Madelyn. Madelyn, home by choice with two small boys with round eager faces, had been a school psychologist and educator, and she took our anxieties, fears and frustrations, as well as our hopes and our dreams for ourselves and our children, seriously. With Madelyn's guidance and under her leadership our informal chats grew into hopeful, life affirming debate sessions which changed people's lives. Some of us took our first steps toward looking at the meaning and significance of our daily struggles, and others of us climbed painstakingly up the stairs towards improving our own self esteem and challenging the careless, sloppy, and faithless way our society viewed children and child rearing.

Today, ten years later, that core group of mothers have moved on into various fields in the work force: teaching, nursing, family therapy, sculpture, retail and so on. Regardless of where our days have led us, the impact of those conversations has never left. Madelyn's wisdom and vision, and unwavering belief in our ability to solve our problems while honoring our children, have been invaluable tools for every aspect of our lives. When

Madelyn and her family moved to Texas we mourned our loss, but over the years we have cheered her successes and applauded the way she has moved out into a much larger community to share her message.

I consider Madelyn to be one of those visionary mentors - not just someone who helped me cope with today, but someone who helped me build for the future. To those of you just opening this book and meeting Madelyn for the first time - breathe a sigh of relief. There is much common sense good advice here; there is much caring, love, and respect in these words. And, most importantly, there is Madelyn's wisdom and her faith in you. Believe in it. Believe in your own ability to find a vision which will help you build strong and resilient bonds with the children in your lives.

Victoria Ryland Mathies

Contents

THE JOURNEY BEGINS

We're all in this together ... alone. - Lily Tomlin

When my oldest son first started drawing, he drew a picture of me as the perfect mom with blonde hair, red cheeks, a smile, and a sun shining brightly. (You see, I am a good mother.) On the other side of that paper, he drew a different version of me. This one had green and white scraggly hair, a zigzag line for a mouth, and no sun. (The real me?) In truth, I was both; he, in his naiveté, had captured my essence. Clearly, something needed to be done. I did it backwards. I sought skills first, but I could not judge their appropriateness with any tool other than, "Does it work?" I was missing the critical component of an underlying principle or in other words, "What does this technique really teach my child, and is this what I want him to learn?" I continued to be at the mercy of the "experts" who so often disagree. I was not seeking expertise; I was seeking and needing wisdom to help me guide my children to healthy, happy, responsible, humane adulthood.

Being a parent is far more challenging, frustrating, and sometimes discouraging than I ever thought it would or could be. And I was a school psychologist, an early childhood educator, and the wife of a teacher *before* I ever had children of my own. My close friends and I have decided that the difficulty of this challenge is one of the world's best-kept secrets. My journey into this book, the subject of which I have been speaking about and teaching for years, began with the frustration and discouragement I experienced as our first-born began toddlerhood. I had never planned to be the *perfect* parent; I had just expected that with all my experience with other people's children and my education (please don't laugh, I was young), I would, at least, be a good parent. Not necessarily so.

I recognized two factors in my poor parenting. First, and most importantly, what I *practiced* and what I *believed* were two different things. My integrity - that elusive ability to match believed principles with practiced principles - was not intact. I constantly found myself dealing with my son much more *nastily* and harshly than I wished. Further, I found myself using practices I knew were not right or helpful. I did not wish to teach my children practices or ideas in which I did not truly believe, yet that is exactly what I found myself doing. Secondly, I simply did not have enough skills, strategies, nor techniques to be a helpful, healthy parent. Neither did I know how to evaluate and select techniques. I needed to learn more, much more. Most jobs or positions require training; generally, the more complicated the job, the longer the training needs to be. Well, it does not get more complex than parenting. Many of us went to college for years to qualify for our occupations, and if we are honest, we admit to having needed on-the-job practice in our fields before we really became skilled. Too often, parents tackle the job of parenting with little or no training and expect themselves to be skilled from the start. This is not only unfair, but also unrealistic.

Discipline, using the term loosely here, has for years now focused heavily on behavior only. When I first started working with children, I, like most teachers and parents, believed discipline is what you do with children to get them to behave. Is this not what you have been taught? This view, however, is short-sighted, out-dated, and, quite frankly, dangerous. Somewhere in our minds, we must be able to envision our child on his or her sixteenth birthday. I know where she will be - at the Department of Motor Vehicles seeking freedom in the form of a driver's license. By that time, the correct principles (responsibility, responsiveness, respect, etc.) must be in place. These principles will help determine how each new driver decides to operate a car. Will she drive the speed limit only when there are police around? Will she drive fast because it is fun? Or, will she understand that *how she chooses to operate the vehicle will determine whether people live or die?* It is critical that each driver understands this last statement. The safety of each of our children and loved ones depends on it.

How we discipline a child at age two, at age five, at age nine, plays a significant role in determining how he drives at sixteen, how he handles relationships, what kind of spouse and parent he becomes, in short, how he handles his life. Thus, discipline cannot afford to be short-sighted and look merely at how to most quickly and efficiently get a child to behave now. Certainly we do not want to give up immediate effectiveness; we need to be effective. Immediate effectiveness is not enough. We need to build on this layer and move into a higher level of discipline. This next level looks at what lesson needs to be learned and how best to teach it to a specific child. What principles are involved? Do I believe in these principles? Fundamental to this program is the principle of responsibility for actions. Every child and every adult needs to understand and believe:

I am responsible for what I choose to do and for what happens to me and others as a result of my decisions and actions.

Teaching the ownership of behavior is where we need to be headed. Responsibility for decisions and actions is essential to self-discipline, the final goal. With the rise in the "don't blame me" syndrome, and the "victim" or "something or someone made me do it" defense, teaching responsibility for our actions is decidedly necessary. This is the only place we need to be in full agreement. This responsibility for behavior, the hallmark of self-discipline, is the vision or path upon which the techniques are based. The individual techniques and strategies we choose will vary with personality, values, child, and situation.

Yes, you can be the parent you want to be, or at least a whole lot closer to it. And yes, being a family can be mostly healthy, happy, and a benefit to you, rather than a detriment to your life. It is critical not only for our own sanity and our children's lives, but also for our future, that we learn to guide our children through childhood and into healthy adulthood. There is so much they need to learn and know about in order to become emotionally healthy, happy, functional adults: healthy relationships, sound and helpful communication, correct principles to guide their lives, problem solving, responsiveness to others, respect, responsibility for actions, resourcefulness, negotiating skills, self-esteem, dealing with anger. It is clear we must not only be knowledgeable in these areas, but we must also know positive ways to teach them.

The task is large, but not impossible. The benefits more than offset the effort and struggle. After all, what are emotionally healthy, responsible, contributing adults worth? What is a child with high self-esteem worth? What are respectful, responsible teens worth? What is a life long bond with each of your children worth?

Teaching, working with children, is a most noble profession. It is also mentally and emotionally taxing. Veteran teachers across North America describe changes (decreases in self-esteem, respect, self-discipline, motivation; and increases in anger, emotional disturbance, aggression, apathy) which have made teaching more difficult. As is true with parenting, teaching is challenging and at times can be more frustrating and discouraging than we envisioned. Most of us began our careers wanting simply to teach and quickly discovered we needed effective disciplinary tools in order to get to the teaching.

In addition, we may not have considered the need to support and supplement the parents. This particular role has always been part of a teacher's job. From the beginning there have been orphaned, neglected, abused, and needy children. Sadly, their number is multiplying at a remarkable rate. Despite the increase in this population, teachers must continue to be role models and provide discipline. Although school is not the last chance for troubled children, it is the last easy chance.

Entering and remaining in this profession is a choice; the task is large, but not impossible. The emotional benefits can be tremendous. Christa McAuliff said it beautifully, "I touch the future. I teach." Most respectfully I would add, "I touch lives; I teach." Teaching can be the profession you had hoped for, and you can be the teacher you have always wanted to be.

Let us begin by developing a guiding vision.

PART I - VISION

1:
A Rope Across the River

In his book, *The Seven Habits of Highly Effective People*, Stephen Covey addresses the need for leaders in the business world to have vision - a sense of where they are headed. He describes it as "begin with the end in mind." In fact, anyone in a leadership position, this includes parents and teachers, *must* have vision.

He tells a great story about the importance of vision and the difference between managers, who do things right, and leaders, who do the right things. He tells of a group of workers cutting through the jungle to make a road. They are making great progress, thanks to their managers' organization and support and the workers' skills. However, a leader arrives and decides to climb a tree just to make sure they are on course. It turns out they are not only on the wrong course, but they are also in the wrong jungle. Not unlike the WWII pilot who reported, "I don't know where I am, but I'm making record time." We neither want, nor can we afford, to make record time on a path into destruction, dysfunction, or invalid principles with our children. We need to be leaders with a clear vision.

Without question, we as parents are in the most important position of leadership. Teachers, similarly, are clearly the leaders of their classrooms. Vision becomes not only a critical skill, but also a guiding factor. And directions are certainly helpful. Guiding factors have been missing from discipline for too long. Vision is like a rope tossed across a river with a strong current, that when firmly attached to the other side, helps us arrive where we want, rather than where the current chooses to take us. Many parents and teachers have been trying to cross the river with no rope. They inevitably end up *somewhere* down river feeling cold, wet, and tired. With the rope as a guide, tied securely to a tree directly across the river, we can cross the river and *arrive where we wanted!* We will still occasionally feel cold, wet, and tired, but no corrective measures will be required, for we will have made it to our chosen destination.

Where we are now: The state of America's children

> As the family goes, so goes the nation and so goes the whole world in which we live.   - Pope John Paul II

It is not just individual people who are lost. Our nation is in desperate need of corrective measures. For too many years, both parents and teachers have disciplined without vision, without the necessary guidance and leadership. We have allowed ourselves to be completely engaged fighting fires. Not only have adults and children suffered, but our nation has paid a tremendous price. The United States is currently the most violent country in the industrialized world; we rather notoriously lead in the number of homicides, assaults, and rapes.[1] In 1993, it was reported that gun-related violence took the life of a child every three hours, that is 25 children, a classroom full, every three days.[2] In 1994, the Children's Defense Fund reported that a child dies from gun-related violence once every two hours, or a classroom full every two days. And gun-related violence is still increasing. Further, ninety-one percent of responding teachers reported increased violence among children in their classrooms.[3] In its "The State of American Children Yearbook 1994," the Children's Defense Fund described One Day in the Life of American Children:

3	Children die from child abuse
9	Children are murdered
13	Children die from guns
30	Children are wounded by guns
202	Children are arrested for drug offenses
307	Children are arrested for crimes of violence
340	Children are arrested for drinking or drunken driving
1,234	Children run away from home
2,255	Teenagers drop out of school each day
2,781	Teenagers get pregnant
5,314	Children are arrested for all offenses
5,703	Teenagers are victims of violent crime
7,945	Children are reported abused or neglected
1,200,000	Latchkey children come home to houses in which there is a gun

In order to help redirect our nation back on track, *we must stop viewing discipline as simply what we do to get children to behave.* That is, to change their behavior right now. This viewpoint, this paradigm, is very short-sighted and dangerous. Our discipline techniques must include ideas about where we want to be in the future, what type of child-teen-adult we want, and need, in the long run. Perhaps you've heard the saying: "The cure for crime is not found in the electric chair, but in the high chair." Nothing could be more true today. We must begin with this end in mind, or we will, as a nation, flounder in the cold, swift-moving river of life.

Unfortunately, for many parents and teachers, there appear to be no ropes available to assist them in crossing the river of parenthood. But are there? Certainly. Our correct principles are the guiding ropes. It is our correct principles which we must identify and use. Again, it is Stephen Covey who provides the background ideas about principles:

Principles are guidelines for human conduct that are proven to have enduring, permanent value. They're fundamental.... Principles are not *values.* A gang of thieves can share values, but they are in violation of the fundamental principles we're talking about. Principles are the territory. Values are maps. When we value correct principles, we have truth - a knowledge of things as they are.

Principles include *fairness, honesty, integrity, respect, responsibility, resourcefulness, responsiveness, humaneness, perseverance, and excellence.* They are like our Constitution. They are the guiding lights that help keep us focused and on track. They do not change. We all recognize their benefit. For example, whether pro-life or pro-choice, we all believe in the principle that human life has value. The disagreement begins when we interpret a principle as a value. Those who favor the *value* (interpretation of principle) of pro-choice believe strongly in the worth of a mother's life. Those who favor the *value* of pro-life believe strongly in the worth of an unborn baby's life. The point is that the fundamental principle - a strong belief in the worth of human life - is the same starting point for both groups. I have worked with thousands of parents and educators; they continue to agree on some core correct principles; of course, they disagree frequently on values.

Some adults, many youth, and the criminal element of our population fail to value correct principles. They operate on flawed principles. These include unfairness, only working toward one's own advantage, dishonesty, lack of respect, blaming others for one's behavior and mistakes, and so forth. Neither do some of these people recognize the principle that human life is valuable. As individuals and as a nation, we continue to pay for flawed principles. It is absolutely critical that we help children develop the correct principles to guide their lives and aid their decisions.

Another way to look at principles, specifically with regard to discipline, is to ask what principles does any technique or group of techniques teach. Clearly, we want to be teaching principles we believe in, principles we want used with us as we age, and principles upon which we want our nation and future built. In other words, are we teaching correct or flawed principles? Wise or unwise principles? Beneficial or harmful principles? The Law of the Harvest - we reap what we sow - is always operating. Our tomorrow is sown today. It is helpful, then, to examine the underlying principles of the four most common systems of child-rearing. In so doing, we will discover what they teach our children and, accordingly, whether or not we want to use them. We will also see how the way we have managed children in the past has contributed to our present.

2:
What Do I Want to Teach?

We must believe the things we teach our children.
- Woodrow Wilson

Control - Power

The first system we will explore is a system based on control. By control I mean that thumbs-pressed-down-on-them, autocratic, brute force (either by physical or verbal superiority) way of dealing with children. In a word - Power. Those of us who have an audio-tape playing in our heads which tells us, "good parents control their children," or "good teachers control their classrooms," qualify. During the holidays, at the Thanksgiving dinner table with your parents and relatives present, can you hear this recording? Or as a teacher, do you hear this tape when the principal walks by your classroom? Are you a bottom-line, get things done efficiently, productive person? Do you prefer to have situations under control? These personality types and values are not wrong or bad; however, we need to consider where this principle of Power may lead us and what it teaches children.

CONTROL - POWER	
Belief	Question Asked by Child
Good parents control their children. Good teachers control their classrooms. ⇨	"Who will make me?"
Good kids always behave. ⇨	"Make me!"

Two problems occur when we consistently use power to get our way with children. First, children determine that in families, in classrooms, in life, it is fair and right to use power to get one's way. We, the older generation, can be very short-sighted; for inevitably, the balance of power will shift from us and return to haunt us. I do not wish to be removed from my home against my will by my children. If I teach power as a way of operating, as an acceptable method of dealing with people, I am foolish not to expect power to be used against me (Law of the Harvest). Second, many children learn from our modeling exactly how to wield power. They become tyrants in their own right. As these children enter adolescence, they rebel harshly. Some of us live with two-year olds who understand and love power (**NO!**). But as tyrants age, they can and do make family life extremely difficult and unpleasant. They seem to bring out the worst in all of us. They also frequently grow up to become autocratic heads of a new family and pass on this dysfunctional style of interaction.

Be aware, many children by personality or inclination seem to thrive on power from an early age. Two's, five's and thirteen's are in developmental stages which include separation and finding one's own identity. These stages typically include the wielding of power, yet they are necessary parts of growing up. Wielding power against these children aggravates an already present proclivity or personality.

Some children learn a different lesson from being controlled. They learn the opposite end of control - submission. In order for one person to dominate, another must become submissive. Do you want submissive children? (I know, sounds lovely in theory, and some of you are thinking a little submission would be nice.) Submission is, as we have learned of late, a very dangerous lesson to learn. There are many men and women who have learned this lesson well. However, it is women who have been the focus of concern most recently. It is clear from the need for Women's Shelters all over our country that too many women learned the lesson of submission. If they married emotionally healthy spouses, they only have trouble saying "no" to volunteer work or to their children. If, however, they married emotionally unhealthy spouses, they are being abused physically and emotionally as you read this. Children and adults tend either to believe that they are victims and things happen to them or to believe that they are in charge of their lives and have control over the direction their lives take. Do you want to risk your child? In the section on self-esteem, we will discuss more thoroughly the loss of self-esteem linked to submission, helplessness, and victimization.

It is important to consider what a child schooled in power and control asks himself when he is deciding how to behave. "Who's going to make me?" is typical. My younger son was stronger than me when he was eleven. Had we taught power as a principle of operation, I would have been in trouble this early in his life. Consider this potential scenario: I tell him it is his turn to empty the dishwasher. He replies, "Who's going to make me?" and I have to answer, "Your dad when he gets home." Not my idea of fine discipline! As he gets older and stronger still, he turns the question into a statement, "Make me." Dad will also be older, and be less able to make him.

When the drug dealer approaches this type of child and offers drugs, the child's question becomes, "Who's going to stop me?" Parents will likely not be present during this offer, nor will there be a teacher or police officer around. Successful drug dealers avoid the latter with skill. *There is not going to be anyone to stop her.* And the chain of substance abuse is started. Another significant question to ask is how does this child drive? Very, very well - when she sees a police car. As she pleases (and frequently in rebellion), when she sees that the policeman has pulled someone else over and that the odds are slim to none that there is another officer on this same street. There is *no one around to make her* drive the right speed through your school zone. Does the phrase, "no cop, no stop" ring a bell?

So what do we know? *Power*, for many of us, is seductively tempting. Who doesn't like things his way? But a system of child management based on control teaches dangerous lessons and is based on the flawed principle of power. Is this the legacy you want to leave - "My way or the highway!" Or do you want something more for your child(ren)? And, since it is sometimes difficult to tell who will seize the idea of power and run with it and who will learn submission, do you want to teach lessons which may prove very harmful and unhealthy for your child? Healthy families are not built on the foundation of power.

Yes, there is a time for control. Life-threatening situations may call for power. Situations where emotional health is involved also call for immediate action. A parent can and should place a child in drug rehabilitation or residential treatment when needed, or physically remove a child from danger. But please keep in mind, picking up the toys or taking out the garbage is not a life-threatening situation.

What price has our nation paid? The use of "power without discipline" is increasing dramatically. There was a time when attainment of power - political, financial, physical, or influential - was accompanied by the development of self-discipline. Money accrued through hard work. The martial arts take years and years to master. Wise, respected, respectable leaders mature through years of experience. Not so any more. Money is stolen. Political office can be bought. Physical power over others is just one handgun away. The procuring of power without the development of self-discipline is not only possible, it is too easy.

The price exacted is reflected by our number one ranking in violence in the industrialized world. Sexual harassment is also a form of use of power without discipline. Abuse of power riddles both private enterprise and the public sector. When we add physical, emotional, and sexual abuse, the toll is staggering.

Each of us must decide what principles we choose to use and teach. We must decide whether short-term or long-term gain is more important. And we must each foresee that we will reap what we have sown.

Rewards & Bribes: Behavior Modification

When I was in graduate school, B.F. Skinner, the founder of operant conditioning and thus, reward systems, was considered a giant in the field of psychology. During my college career, I took a graduate-level course focused solely on reinforcement theory and practice, and as a result set up numerous reinforcement programs for school children. Now, despite its founder's concerns and new understanding in the past decade, this system continues to be found in many books and schools. As we look at reward systems, the appeal will become clear, as will the dangers. Two facts must be remembered. First, Dr. Skinner was a brilliant man who made major contributions to our body of knowledge. Second, the laws regarding rewards and punishment (operant learning theory) which he discovered and described are true and operate regardless of whether or not we are aware of them. And we need to be aware of them.

REWARDS & BRIBES	
Belief	Question Asked by Child
Rewarded behavior repeats itself. ⇨	"What will I get?"
⇨	"What's in it for me?"

Many parents and teachers continue to believe that giving a child a reward is innocent, even nice. After all, it can feel good to both parties involved. The audio tape we play to ourselves here is, "What can I use to get this kid to behave?" But if we look with a more thoughtful eye, we can see how clear underlying principles would help us decide what is appropriate and helpful.

Most of us, especially those in education, have been taught that the purpose of rewarding behavior is to increase the probability of that behavior's return - to get a child to do something favorable again (use the toilet, not talk in class). Rewards work in theory and practice with both animals and people. Usually, when we reward a child's behavior, the child does repeat the behavior again. This, in turn, *rewards us* and makes us believe we are being effective. What we overlook is that we have to continue to reward more and more frequently as children become dependent on reinforcement. Eventually, they begin to believe that the world owes them, and they expect to be rewarded for any and all good behavior. As well, we quickly discover that what was once motivating is no longer; we are forced to increase the value of the reward. Children begin to operate on the flawed principle of greed. They require more and more and bigger and bigger. If we look down the road this is what we see. We view the high school student who gets paid for grades or gets a car for a year of good grades. We find a 14 year old who says he is not going to take out the trash because he already has enough money to go the movies on Saturday. We have adolescents searching for the now-elusive kick one receives with a great reward and finding it in drugs, alcohol, promiscuity, and sadly, even violence.

Were you paid to fix dinner or to do the dishes last night? If not (and none of us were), we need to ask ourselves if we want our children to operate under a different system and set of principles than we do; often we do, indeed, pay children to do household chores.[4] It must be clear in our minds why we did the dishes for no pay; we must recognize the principles upon which we base our lives. We chose to do dishes for no pay because everyone over the age of two needs to contribute to the family unit; no one has the right to be a parasite. No matter what group we belong to (family, classroom, nation), we must help maintain or improve it. Groups cannot stay alive without this principle. It is part of belonging. Too many parasites and the group falters and may not survive.

What else do rewards teach? Rewards teach external motivation at the expense of internal motivation. Rewards teach that it is *our* job to motivate them, rather than *their* job to motivate themselves. When we place a carrot in front of a child, she focuses on the carrot rather than on the important internal motivators such as feeling good with a job well done, learning something, or accomplishing something. These internal motivators are far more powerful and longer-lasting. Teachers, especially secondary teachers, often ask me, "How can we motivate these students who have become so dependent on rewards and external motivation?" This question takes us in the wrong direction; it keeps us searching for outside motivators. The more helpful question is, "How can we increase intrinsic motivation? How can we help them motivate themselves?" Rewards, as a form of external motivation, prevent or destroy internal motivation. It is very difficult to even consider why something makes us feel good inside when there is always a carrot out in front of us demanding our attention. We give them class work to do and they ask, "What will I get?" We fail to answer with the truth, "Smarter, that is why your parents send you to school!"

Internal motivators are the true building blocks for self-esteem. Repeatedly we have been told we need to reward children to build self-esteem. This is not so. In fact, rewards and praise (verbal reinforcement) frequently do more damage to self-esteem than good. They focus on only one area of self-esteem and do harm to the other two areas. Please see "Over-Emphasis on Accomplishment" and "Praise" in Part IV on Self-Esteem for a more thorough discussion of praise.

This leads us directly to a related concern. Reinforcement or rewards also prevent children from developing a good sense of evaluation. An adult is always in charge of determining what is good enough, what deserves a reward. Do you know someone who will not select an outfit without another's aid and approval? Evaluating issues and candidates is an important skill for voters. Democracies require adults who can evaluate. Children who do not practice evaluating themselves have difficulty developing this vital skill. Even as adults, they are unable to say to themselves, "I did well - I was great!" without confirmation from someone else. Clearly, being unable to say "well-done!" to yourself limits self-esteem. Do we want to teach children to look for a pat on the back or is it more helpful to teach them to pat themselves on the back? Please see Part IV on Self-Esteem for changing praise to descriptive appreciation and teaching children to pat themselves on the back.

In addition, rewards teach immediate gratification - "I want what I want now." Do you know anyone currently in trouble with credit cards because he had to have something right now despite the checkbook balance? Deferred gratification is indeed a virtue and a sign of maturity. Deferred gratification helps us wait with grace.

For years we have overlooked a hidden factor in reward systems. They are by nature manipulative. Webster's Seventh New Collegiate Dictionary defines manipulate as "to control or play upon by artful, unfair, or insidious means especially to one's own advantage." When we determine what behaviors we want, when we shape behavior and mold children without their consent or knowledge to our own advantage, we are, by definition, manipulating. The words we use to describe these concepts are generally quite revealing and accurate. Consider *behavior management* and *behavior modification.* Do you want your behavior managed or modified, probably without your understanding of what is being done to you? Do you want to teach manipulation as a skill to your children? Research and experience repeatedly inform us that our modeling - our actions, what we do - is the best, most powerful teaching tool. Use manipulation, teach manipulation, and expect to be manipulated in turn. (Law of the Harvest, once again.) One of the most common complaints I hear about reward systems is that children frequently manipulate them to their advantage. Quick learners!

In addition, we must consider our own aging and the increasing vulnerability which will accompany it. News accounts of senior citizens being manipulated and swindled are all too common. The trend of elderly parents being left to fend for themselves, often after having turned over their financial assets to their adult children, is quite disturbing. Any form of elder abuse is distressing; and we are witnessing increasing amounts of it.

Do you like to be manipulated by others? No one does. The next question to ask yourself is do you believe in the Golden Rule: "Do unto others as you would have them do unto you." If you do not like to be manipulated and do believe in the Golden Rule, then your integrity is jeopardized by using reward systems. For another way to phrase the Golden Rule is: do you choose to treat others in ways you do not wish to be treated? For our own integrity, we must treat children as we wish to be treated.

Lastly, what question do reward systems teach children to ask when they are deciding how to behave? "What will I get?" or the more sophisticated version, "What's in it for me?" This is harmful to individual children, as well as to our nation. First, the drug dealer has a response to "What's in it for me?" It is, "You're going to feel wonderful - better than you've ever felt before (temporary replacement of real self-esteem); it's going to happen right away (immediate gratification). Trust me (no evaluation skills). And, if I decide I like you (manipulation), you can make more money (the world owes me) in one night with me than both your parents do in two months (greed)." All of this sounds mighty good to this child. And, again, we lose another child down the path of illicit drug use and addiction.

Our nation has paid a huge price for the use of these flawed principles, and not just in terms of increased drug use and related crimes. B. F. Skinner reportedly spent the last years of his life explaining to people that if we continue to treat children like rats (manipulation), they will indeed become rats. And, that if we continue to use rewards as a major form of child management, our nation will reduce its ability to function as a democracy. Some citizens lack the ability to evaluate candidates, issues, and policies. The "what's in it for me" attitude is identifiable. Too often individual interest prevails over community interest. Too many allow themselves to be driven by the question, "What's in it for me?" They fail to ask the more important questions such as, "Is this good for the family? For the community? For the future?" or "Is someone else in greater need?" A democratic government cannot survive too many special interests and not enough best interest for all.

Healthy individuals do not develop from rewards and the harmful principles that they teach. Families, classrooms, and democratic nations require healthy individuals. Rewards are dangerously and seductively short-sighted. Again, each of us must determine what we choose to teach.

Punishment

> No more tears now; I will think upon revenge. - Mary Stuart, Queen of Scotland

Punishment is not truly a separate system; it operates under the same learning principles as behavior management. However, punishment is an ancient system. It is helpful to look at punishment separately, as an entity itself. "This child is going to pay," is the audio tape those of us who lean toward punishment hear in our minds.

PUNISHMENT		
Belief		Question Asked by Child
"There's nothing wrong with this child that a good lickin' wouldn't fix."	⇨	"Is it worth it?"
"This child is going to pay."	⇨	"Who's looking?"

We cannot ignore inappropriate behavior; certainly a lesson must be taught. But there is a difference between hurting emotionally or physically to teach a lesson and simply teaching a lesson. *Punishment is different from discipline.* The definitions of punish include: 1) to inflict a penalty...in retribution, 2) to deal with roughly or harshly, 3) to inflict injury upon, 4) hurt. Punishment, by definition, is doing something ugly or hurtful to another because we do not like what he did. Discipline is teaching - period.

The first concern about punishment involves the lessons it teaches. First, we teach children that when they do not do what we want, we have the right to hurt them either physically or emotionally. None of us had children so we could damage them. And when not threatened, do others have the right to hurt us? As stated earlier, our nation is currently ranked first among industrialized nations in violence. Too many people believe they have the right to hurt another because they do not like what someone else does or looks like or has. And yes, we want to teach children what is appropriate and what is not, or that a digression is quite serious or must never be repeated. *There are many excellent discipline tools which not only accomplish these lessons without needing punishment, but also teach them more effectively.*

Second, punishment is something negative we <u>do</u> to children, such as take away an *unrelated* privilege, or hurt them physically or emotionally to improve behavior. It need not be fair or just. Punishment creates resentment. Resentment results in people working *<u>against</u>* one another. A significant component of healthy families is their ability and desire to work <u>with</u> one another, to trust that the others will operate with every member's best interests at heart. Punishment works in contradiction to this important method of operating. No form of child management works well or easily when a child consistently chooses to work against us. Creating resentment makes our job far more difficult.

Third, research and experience show us that punishment is not effective. Results are temporary, short-term. Parents have to continuously punish. This is *spend discipline* at its worst, and in complete contrast to *investment discipline*. As a parent, I want to do less and less discipline as my children get older (investment discipline). Teachers, as well, want to do less, not more and more (spend discipline) as the school year progresses. As children age, we want to see fewer incidents requiring us to discipline them and ever increasing incidents where they discipline themselves (self-discipline).

In addition, a punishment that once worked soon fails, and something harsher and nastier must replace it. In order for punishment to work, we need to be increasingly cruel and hurtful until we have done enough damage to hurt self-esteem and to create victims. It is easy to see how parents can be tricked into believing that hitting works. A slight, innocuous tap on a three year old often produces desired results quickly; the child improves his behavior. As a result, this parent is reinforced or rewarded for striking her child. The parent, at wit's end, believes she has finally found something that works. The parent's belief that hitting works is strongly reinforced. But teenagers do not respond to a small tap; they require a much more severe blow to get results. It is also easy to understand how with no other skills to fall back on this parent has trapped herself into levelling a blow to the head to get a fifteen year old to behave. Thus we perceive how a parent who unknowingly or unwittingly began to change her young child's behavior with a very small tap is, over the years, lulled and seduced into hitting harder and harder. Bear in mind, calling a three-year old naughty may help improve his behavior, but much stronger and uglier words will be needed for an older child or adolescent. Damage to self-esteem occurs from the first put-down. Sooner or later, the small belittling grows to verbal and emotional abuse. Again, parents travel down a steadily steeper path into harm.

The questions that frequently punished children ask themselves when they choose how to behave are, "Who's looking?" "Will I get caught?" and "Is it worth it?" Frequently, the answers are respectively, "No one," "Probably not," and "Probably." These children need *constant* monitoring. They do not own their behavior; they just pay for it - occasionally. When the drug dealer approaches these children, they look around to see if there is a police officer nearby. If not, they feel free to go ahead. After all, "I'll never get caught" is a common belief system of adolescents. Let us imagine this child driving through your school zone. As he enters, he ponders, "Who's looking?" (probably no one who can arrest him), "Will I get caught?" (probably not), and "Is it worth it?" (probably, it's only a ticket). "So why not?" Using these flawed principles, there is no reason to slow down.

Lastly, let us address the common question, "Shouldn't people pay for what they have done?" It depends on what is meant by pay. Live with fair consequences, make amends, learn the lesson involved - these are forms of helpful discipline. If these are your idea of pay, then the answer is yes. But if by pay you mean suffer violence, be hurt emotionally, feel vengeful, then the answer is no. Mean, evil, wicked people can pay - be punished - despite the fact that sociologists have long recognized that even severe punishment is seldom a deterrent. Murderers, rapists, perpetrators of heinous crimes can pay for their evil deeds. But children who misbehave (do not pick up their toys) are neither criminals nor evil people. Children need to *learn*. Our job as parents is not to warp or damage them, but to guide them to health. Criminals pay; children learn - so the children will not need to pay as adults or as criminals.

☞ When a child does cross over into severely maladaptive or malicious behavior, the child and his family are in need of immediate psychological help and intervention. (Seek professional diagnosis if you are unsure.)

What price has our nation paid? There are increasing, almost unbelievable numbers of abused children today. The Children's Defense Fund's "The State of America's Children Yearbook 1994" listed 2,695,010 children reported abused or neglected. Which is worse - emotional or physical abuse? I do not know. They both destroy - one the soul, the other the body. As a nation, we must stop teaching children that violence is acceptable; we must stop teaching that one person has the right to hurt another because he does not like what he does; and we must stop teaching that violence is an acceptable way to solve problems. We are finally beginning to accept that men and women do not have the right to strike or abuse one another. When will we extend this protection to children? We can neither condone nor continue the violence done to our children. It is this generation's responsibility, *our* responsibility to stop passing on pain, abuse, and violence. We must become a transition figure - someone who stops the transmission of negative tendencies from one generation to the next.

Discipline - The Road Less Traveled

> Two roads diverged in a wood, and I -
> I took the one less traveled by,
> and that has made all the difference.
>   - Robert Frost, "The Road Not Taken"

What type of discipline system can accomplish what we need? What is our vision, our path? It is discipline in its original meaning. The root word of discipline is *disciplina*, meaning teaching, learning. Disciple (learner) stems from the same word. Discipline at first meant the teaching or guidance we give to children. Discipline involved lessons: life lessons, lessons in correct principles, lessons in respectful communication, lessons in healthy relationships. It did not mean make them behave so we look good. It did not mean pay them to be good. It did not mean make them pay. *It recognized that children arrive in this world uncivilized and require substantial instruction.* What is the most fundamental principle we need to teach?

You are responsible for what you choose to do and for what happens to you and others as a result of your decisions and actions.

DISCIPLINE		
Belief		Question Asked by Child
Self-discipline is the goal.	⇨	"Is this a right or good thing for me to do?"
You are responsible for what you choose to do and for what happens as a result.	⇨	"What could happen if I choose to do this?"

> To be a man is to be responsible. - Antoine de Saint-Exupéry

Self-discipline is what we seek to bestow upon our children, the ability to discipline themselves, to base their decisions on outcomes, to own their actions. For, sooner or later, we will not be around to discipline them, and they must pick up this critical task themselves.

A child who has been brought up with this type of system learns to ask himself, "Is this a right or good thing for me to do? What could possibly happen if I choose to do this?" These questions guide children to think ahead to consequences and effects rather than just immediate behavior. As well, they help place ownership of actions squarely where they belong - with the child.

When a drug dealer approaches a child who asks himself these questions, the answers (prison, loss of everyone and everything valued, death) completely foil the drug dealer. The drug dealer does not stand a chance, but our children and our nation do.

A true DISCIPLINE (using the term strictly from here on) system leads to self-discipline, is based on correct principles, is investment discipline, and constitutes **DISCIPLINE FOR LIFE**. This system teaches each child what he or she needs to learn to function as an emotionally healthy, humane, responsible adult and changes behavior, as well.

Fortunately, each child arrives with some life lessons already or nearly learned. Some children will never be helpless victims. They look after themselves and their needs without being taught. They seem intuitively to know that they can think and do for themselves. The other side of the coin is that these children frequently need to learn sensitivity and awareness of others. Another group is much more vulnerable to helplessness. Still others seem innately to recognize and consider other people's feelings and needs. We do not need to teach them responsiveness or empathy. Still others seem to more easily accept ownership of actions; their counterparts fight it tooth and nail. Why do children arrive in this world in so many different guises? I believe it is one of life's little jokes on us. Any parent of more than one child and every teacher recognizes these two truths (or jokes on us) about children. First, *no two children are alike*. Some are easy; some more difficult. Some are like us; some are very different. Each has a different personality, different skills, and different strengths and weaknesses. In short, each child has different life lessons to learn. And secondly, each learns differently. Thus life's second joke is that *what works with one child does not necessarily work with another*. We need many, many skills, and we must be adept with each. We must be extremely skilled to accommodate any given child, let alone a number of them.

Understanding the features of a true DISCIPLINE system will help us.

ONE GOAL FOR DISCIPLINE

1 Goal for Discipline	Lead to SELF-DISCIPLINE • by providing opportunities for learning • by allowing the child to be and feel responsible for his behavior "What lesson needs to be learned here; how can I best teach it to this child?"

The goal for discipline then is to teach children and to lead them increasingly toward self-discipline. We do this by regarding misbehavior as opportunities for our teaching and their learning. (Of course, sometimes the opposite occurs.) Further, we not only allow but encourage or cause a child to be and to feel responsible for his behavior. Discipline first and foremost asks the question,

What lesson needs to be learned here; how can I best teach it to this child?

Notice that it does not start with the now more common question, "How can I get this child to behave?" This is the mistake we have made for far too long. We have focused only on changing behavior. We have judged our success only by how quickly behavior changed. We forgot about lessons. We forgot about correct principles. And we forgot about the future.

TWO INGREDIENTS OF DISCIPLINE

2 Ingredients of Discipline	Maintain the DIGNITY - of both parties • by using the Golden Rule and Respectful Language Require AUTHORITY - • "Don't start what you can't finish!" • Say what you mean; Mean what you say; Take action stated

Two essential components of discipline are: maintaining respect and carrying authority. Treating children with respect is another way of describing maintaining dignity. It is critical that we safeguard dignity, both our own and the child's, when we discipline a child. Otherwise, we tend to create resistance rather than cooperation. Consider the last time someone treated you disrespectfully - violated your dignity. What was your response? Did you like them less, cooperate less? Perhaps you even chose to work against them - enjoyed working against them? Further, did your self-esteem suffer? To destroy self-esteem is never the goal of discipline. When we add the ingredient of respect to our dealings with our children, we are acting upon the principle of the Golden Rule: "Do unto others as you would have them do unto you." We all want to be treated respectfully. Not only do we experience more cooperation, we model a correct principle. One of my favorite definitions of respect was offered by Bernard Malamud:

"Respect is what you have to have in order to get it."

We will have to give respect before we can expect to receive respect. The next section, "Gaining Cooperation Without Losing Your Mind," addresses using the Golden Rule and Respect as a Second Language.

The second ingredient of discipline is our ability to establish and carry authority, authority based on expertise or position, not power or fear. There is a difference between the unhealthy fear of being hurt emotionally or physically and the healthy fear of what someone you respect will think or feel, or fear of hurting others or oneself.

Authority, however, is necessary for effectiveness. In other words, discipline without authority is ineffective. We cannot afford to be nice but ineffective. "Don't start what you can't finish!" is an important factor in maintaining authority. To be effective in discipline it is critical that we are able to consistently follow through with the three steps to maintaining authority:

Say what you mean - respectfully
Mean what you say - remember what you addressed
Take action stated when necessary

Whenever we do not follow through and finish discipline we have started, we teach our children to test us. This is neither good nor fun for us. Since children don't know whether or not we might follow through on what we have said, they would be foolish not to try to get away with something this time. Earlier it was mentioned that we need to be aware of Skinner's operant conditioning principles functioning in our lives. Here is a prime example from research:

When pigeons were rewarded with food for pecking a certain spot, they learned to peck at the right place when they were hungry. Then the researchers tried to get rid of or extinguish this behavior. The pigeons who had been reinforced at consistent or fixed intervals (every peck, or every 3 pecks, or every 20 pecks) soon gave up. They learned when it was futile to keep trying. However, the researchers found that it was extremely difficult to extinguish pecking behavior with the pigeons who had been intermittently reinforced (food at random intervals - sometimes at 1 peck, sometimes after 13 pecks, sometimes after 5 pecks). These pigeons *never knew when the food would come and thus had no way of learning when it was time to quit or when it was foolish to quit trying.*

Gambling is another excellent example of an intermittently reinforced behavior which can be subsequently difficult to eliminate. When we sometimes follow through and sometimes do not, we place our children in an intermittent reinforcement situation; getting away with something is usually rewarding. The resultant "testing and pushing to the limit" behavior is inordinately difficult to extinguish. It is most helpful to us to follow through each time we discipline and to finish what we start. Testing becomes a pointless and, therefore, foolish thing to do.

Please note that never was it stated that it is necessary to discipline every incident - only that we must follow through with what we started. Choose your battles wisely.

Discipline requires both components: discipline without respect generates resistance, disrespect, and emotional ill health; discipline without authority is not effective.

THREE CRITICAL LIFE BELIEFS

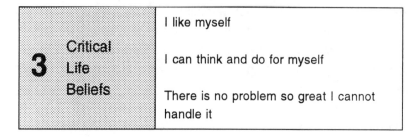

3 Critical Life Beliefs	I like myself
	I can think and do for myself
	There is no problem so great I cannot handle it

Three of the critical life beliefs Barbara Coloroso describes in her seminar are woven throughout this discipline system. Later, when we look at building self-esteem, we will again see the importance of helping children develop these beliefs about themselves. These form the foundation for self-esteem. When discipline is grounded in these beliefs, we build rather than destroy self-esteem with our discipline. None of us had children or chose to work with them to make them feel badly about themselves. How we discipline will be a significant factor affecting self-esteem; for it is during discipline that we are frequently at our worst.

FOUR STEPS TO DISCIPLINE

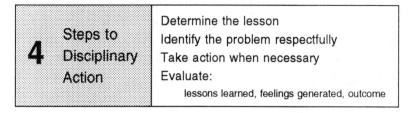

4 Steps to Disciplinary Action	Determine the lesson
	Identify the problem respectfully
	Take action when necessary
	Evaluate:
	lessons learned, feelings generated, outcome

1. Determine the lesson - this is the step that advances discipline beyond the "change behavior now" level and moves it into a higher, more beneficial, long-term level.

This step includes the single most important task anyone does during discipline, ask themselves the question:

> **What lesson needs to be learned here; how can I best teach it to this child?**

Asking this question sets us on the correct path and helps us stay there. We move into investment discipline and DISCIPLINE FOR LIFE. Determining the lesson is absolutely essential.

Asking ourselves what we are about to teach keeps us in the realm of DISCIPLINE FOR LIFE, of true discipline. It is always important to ask this relevant question, or one of its various forms: "What lesson needs to be learned?" or "What life lesson is this child missing here?" or "What flawed principle is this child operating from?" or "What correct principle does this child need to learn?" The answer to any of these questions directs or guides discipline and helps us head in a helpful direction.

2. Identify the problem respectfully and with authority - it is here where we are most likely to create resistance rather than desired cooperation. It is of utmost importance that we think before we speak. We must decide what we want to say (what is the real problem) and how we want to say it (respectfully and assertively).

3. Take the action stated when necessary - this is where we become effective without being nasty. It is also the step we seem to begrudge, despite the fact that we chose to learn much of what we know the hard way, through experience. We did not always listen to our parents and teachers either. (You, of course, immediately stopped seeing a friend or romantic interest the moment your parents disapproved. I don't think so!) Children also choose to learn this way.

4. Evaluate:
- The lessons and principles learned - Did the child learn what was important?
- Feelings generated - How do we both feel?
- Outcome - Was it effective? If it did not work, it does not count for much no matter how good it sounded in theory.

Freedom From Experts - Don't let anyone "should" all over you.

When my children were young, my husband could always tell when I had read another book on child rearing because I would have visibly changed my tactics. I had forgotten that it is my responsibility not just to seek out information, but also to evaluate it. *Each of us is ultimately responsible for how we choose to discipline our children - no one else is or can be.*

I have a very clear memory of a parent in a workshop who was distraught with her teenager whom she could not handle. She was begrudging the fact that spanking no longer worked. In frustration, she said, "But my minister told me to spank; he said it was okay to spank." No one can give you permission; no one else owns this important decision. Only you can give yourself permission. Each of us owns our choices. So let us set ourselves free from the experts forever; let us remove ourselves from any "You should," "You should never," and "Oh, by the way, we're not doing that anymore." We will continue to use the experts for ideas, thoughts, and more rapid understanding - but never for permission or ultimate ownership. The buck, indeed, stops with you.

It is absolutely essential that we are able to judge any system of child rearing and any technique or tip. By slightly altering the question in the first step of discipline, we can accomplish this feat. We need to ask ourselves the following questions: What principle is this system or technique based on? Is this a principle I believe in? Is it a principle that is correct and healthy? Is it a principle I want my child to base his life on? Is this a principle I want to see used in my future? What lessons or life lessons will be learned? If the answers are positive, you can be comfortable and confident in proceeding. If the answers are negative, it is time to look for other solutions.

These questions are helpful in determining which of the experts' ideas and books you value and which you do not find helpful. What we seek is wisdom, not expertise. With these questions, we can find and identify wisdom.

Now - how do we do it?

With a thorough understanding of what discipline is and is not, we have a clearer idea of what we want to achieve with our discipline. We are now ready to discover how to actually accomplish discipline and to learn specific strategies that both teach our principles and are effective.

1 Goal for Discipline	Lead to SELF-DISCIPLINE • by providing opportunities for learning • by allowing the child to be and feel responsible for his behavior "What lesson needs to be learned here; how can I best teach it to this child?"
2 Ingredients of Discipline	Maintain the DIGNITY - of both parties • by using the Golden Rule and Respectful Language Require AUTHORITY - • "Don't start what you can't finish!" • Say what you mean; Mean what you say; Take action stated
3 Critical Life Beliefs	I like myself I can think and do for myself There is no problem so great I cannot handle it
4 Steps to Disciplinary Action	Determine the lesson Identify the problem respectfully Take action when necessary Evaluate: lessons learned, feelings generated, outcome

PART II - GAINING COOPERATION WITHOUT LOSING YOUR MIND!

3:
Barriers to Cooperation

In the first section we looked at the first step of discipline: asking the questions, "What lesson needs to be learned?" and "How can I best teach it?"

Now we examine the second step: the parent or teacher must identify the problem respectfully. We also begin to determine the difference between generating resistance or encouraging cooperation. Frequently, at this early stage of discipline, we inadvertently create resistance. Have you ever noticed that after having said just a few words to a child, you are suddenly in the midst of a power struggle - and all you wanted was for this child to pick up his toys or find a pencil.

Blaming & Accusing	Put-Downs & Belittling	Threats & Intimidation	Commands & Orders	Lecturing & Moralizing
Barriers to Cooperation				
Reminding & Nagging	Guilt	Labeling & Name-Calling	Comparisons	Sarcasm

First, let's look at how we so frequently provoke resistance and defiance. There are many barriers to cooperation; we will identify ten. In the process, we will discover how large a part respect plays in cooperation. We will also determine how many of the ways we have learned to address adults and children hinder more than help us.

> Examples throughout this text appear in the following order and next to the symbols indicated:
>
> ⌂ Parent   ☆ Early Childhood   ● School

As you read through these unhelpful approaches, try to recognize those you say most frequently. After you have discovered which of these you do use, listen for them in your dealings with children. Then observe how much resistance they cause.

Blaming and Accusing[5]

⌂ "You knocked your sister's blocks down."
"You left the car with no gas again; it's always you."

☆ "You pushed him down again, didn't you?"
"You pulled her hair and made her cry."

● "You didn't do your homework, *did* you?"
"You're cheating."

When do we accuse a child of a misdeed? Only when we are absolutely certain that she has done the deed. When we see the child with fresh purple stains on his face, hands, shirt, and pants, we accuse him of having spilled the juice. When there is only one child in the room, we blame that one, of course, for the broken lamp. Yet, if we take a look at what most frequently occurs when *we* are blamed for something, we can more readily see why an accusation creates resistance. If I tell you, "There was entirely too much fat in your dinner last night," you are most likely to answer, "No, there wasn't!" (without even thinking about what you ate). Do you sense resistance in this response? Suddenly, we are in a "prove-it" situation. When we are certain, our job is not to prove it; our job is to deal with it. Another common type of response to this accusation is "So!" or "I enjoyed it immensely." These constitute the "what's-it-to-you" defense. We would not have brought up the situation if it were not important. Suddenly, we are defending why the issue is important rather than dealing with the actual issue. Again, we have come up against resistance. Yet, the older the child, the more likely the prove-it defense, and the more sophisticated. In short, accusing someone is the quickest route to an argument over proof or justification.

An accusation feels like a push; it makes us uncomfortable. We push back or we build a defense. Our first thought is not cooperation. Nor is a child's first response cooperation. Certainly we need to address what has taken place. The point made here is that accusing is not a helpful way to bring up a problem because it most often creates an argument - in other words, resistance.

Put-Downs and Belittling

"Your shoelaces are a disaster. Will you ever learn how to tie your shoes?"
"You call that a clean room?"

"I've never seen anyone dressed like that!"
"Big girls can use the toilet; they don't need diapers."

"Anyone have a better answer?"
"This homework is terrible. I can't even read it."

We are all aware that belittling a child is harmful; it clearly lowers self-esteem. Yet, I have not met a parent or a teacher who has not put down a child - when frustrated, fatigued, or stressed. Put-downs and belittling are well named; we make children feel smaller and less valuable. Trying to regain this lost stature or value, generally and unfortunately at the expense of another, is why we so frequently see a series of put-downs run through the family or a classroom. A child is put-down by someone; as soon as possible, this first child tends to belittle a less powerful child, who in turn puts down an even weaker child. This child may have to kick the family dog or find a younger child on the playground in order to pass off the belittling. The belittling has a life of its own and cycles through the family or school.

We overlook Abraham Lincoln's wisdom that, "You cannot help small men by tearing down big men." Making someone feel or look like less than me only seems to make me look better because everything seems relative. We must take time to teach that having or making someone lower than me does not make me any higher or better. In fact, making someone else feel lower actually reduces me. That's where Booker T. Washington would say, "You can't hold a man down without staying down with him."

Belittling hurts. When someone hurts me, I am less, not more, likely to cooperate. As well, the bond between us is weakened.

☞ Put-downs are easily accomplished without the use of nasty words. A tone can imply disapproval; tone can change respectful words into a put-down. A look alone or accompanied by a gesture easily gives away our feeling. Be very careful; body language, though silent, speaks loudly.

Threats and Intimidation

⌂ "If you touch it again, you're going to be in big trouble."
"If you don't stop it, I'm going to send you to your room."
"Drink and drive one more time, and I won't ever let you use the car."

♣ "If you don't pick up your crayons, I'm going to take them away."
"If you touch that again ...."

🍎 "If you don't start turning in your homework, you're going to fail."
"Forget your book one more time, and I'll give you a zero for the day."
"You're one of my finest art students, maybe the best, but if you don't
    change your behavior in my class, there is absolutely no way I'll even
    consider you for the award for best artist.

Threats are some of my own personal favorites. Each of us has used a threat with a child especially when we feel our backs are up against the wall, when we have tried numerous other strategies which have not worked, or when we finally really mean business.

Some of us have managed to make threats work on occasion. And they can work, especially if we have a big enough menace or punishment at the end and if the child believes we will follow through. However, we must be able to see that what we threaten to do must always continue to grow to be effective. What we can threaten a four year old with will not work with an eleven year old. The threats must get more and more hurtful, *sometimes to the point of physical or emotional harm.* This is not where we are headed legally or morally.

Threats fail to work on many occasions. Some children love to rise to the challenge in a threat; they love to live dangerously as it were. Let us uncover a synonym for threat. When we tell a child, "If you touch that knob one more time, you're going to get it," we can count on almost any child to touch the knob - no matter who she is and even if she had not considered touching the knob again. Generally, if she has any self-respect, she will feel a strong need to touch the knob just one more time - merely to test us. Our threat, our last-ditch effort to stop a behavior, becomes an *invitation* to do exactly what we do not want. A synonym for threat might be invitation.

The threats we have issued previously are not entirely wasted; we can find out about our children's personalities when we threaten them. The aggressive-aggressive child is the one who will look you straight in the eye and touch the knob right away. His actions tell you two things. First, let the game begin and thank you for starting this game because things were boring here for the moment. Second, it is your move. The passive-aggressive child smiles acquiescence and then waits for you to get distracted or busy - which, by the way, takes hardly any time at all. Then she quietly touches the knob and hums some form of "nanny nanny boo boo" and is comforted by the knowledge that she got around you once again. The child who can find the loophole in any situation will touch the knob with her stuffed dog and sweetly tell you that you did not say anything about Rover touching the knob. And a very bright child will touch it as he asks, "Do you mean this one?"

As you can see, what we have determined is that threats easily become invitations to the very behavior we least want. As well, we know that to continually back up our threats, we move more and more closely to harm. In terms of gaining cooperation, threats more often gain us exactly what we did not want.

Threats are often confused with disciplinary consequences where, for example, we tell a child that to continue a behavior (riding a bicycle into the street) will result in a specific consequence (not riding the bike for a day). A threat may be based on the same concept as the disciplinary consequence - that choosing to behave in a certain way (riding the bike into the street) will result in a certain outcome (not riding the bicycle for a time). However, threats are different. To be effective the tone and intent of a threat require power and intimidation. Threats are based in power (if you..., I will....) and punishment (you are going to pay).

In contrast, a consequence seeks to *inform* a child of the disciplinary outcome should the child choose a specific behavior. A consequence does not depend on power, intimidation, or punishment to be effective. *A true disciplinary consequence relies on informed choice.* It is very easy to hear ourselves as offering disciplinary choices and consequences when in fact we are issuing threats. To be sure, 1) check your heart and your intent (to get what you want - control; to make the child pay - punishment), 2) check the child's response (thoughtfulness or continued resistance), and 3) invite another to listen and tell you honestly what she hears. Chapter 7 on Discipline Strategies (page 81) describes disciplinary consequences more fully.

Commands and Orders

⌂ "Get off there NOW!"
   "Stop that!"

⚐ "Don't throw another one."
   "Give it back to him."

🍎 "Put your feet under your desk."
   "Keep your hands to yourself."
   "Hurry up!"

A command, in some ways, seems to be the most direct form of communication: you tell me what to do, and I do it. Pretty simple. Let's just turn it around. I tell *you* what to do and *you* do it. There is the snag. We each want to be the speaker not the doer. Whenever I issue a command ("Stand up!") in a workshop, I obtain various responses. Some participants continue to sit and look at me like I am crazy (aggressive-aggressive). One woman dropped a pencil and said, "Just a minute," (passive-aggressive). Another participant asked, "Do you mean me?"   (bright, very bright). Fortunately, only rarely does someone stand up. I continue to be concerned by these responses. What I have learned is that each one felt uncomfortable with the directive. The rest of the audience empathizes and agrees that they, too, would have been ill at ease. Seldom does a group understand why they are so uneasy with this directive. Perhaps because our dignity is violated more and more often, or perhaps because we try to ignore it when it happens, many of us have lost touch with violation of dignity. For when anyone orders us to do something, our dignity is violated. Not only does self-esteem diminish, but also a sense of defiance develops. We do not like complying with anyone who orders us around. At best, if we are intimidated (perhaps our job depends on this person), we give the letter of the law, not the spirit, in cooperation. And given an opening, we work against this person at every opportunity - maybe even enjoy working against him. *Our children feel the same way.*

No discipline works well or for long when a child chooses to get back at us and work against us. This is an extremely detrimental dynamic and outcome. Families and classrooms deteriorate as a result of this type of toxic relationship. The best analogy for this is the master-slave relationship. Two outcomes are possible: the slaves accept their position and lose dignity and self-respect, or the slaves can choose to rebel and gain back their rightful status and respect. Our children respond exactly the same way. They may accept domination and reduce their own self-worth, or they may rebel and let us know their dignity and self-respect need to be preserved. Unfortunately for us, this important lesson usually sounds like this: "NO!" or "I can't!" or "You can't make me!" or "There's no #*&@ way you can make me!" (the most sophisticated version).   It is still a valid and vital message and lesson to us.

In healthy families and in healthy classrooms, indeed, in any type of healthy relationship, people generally choose to work *with* each other, not *against* each other. It is critical that we learn how to talk to one another and to create this healthy dynamic, not the unhealthy abuse of power and "make me" dynamic. Sooner or later, the abuse of power will return to haunt us. Many of us, including those who do not intend to use power, will be amazed when we listen to ourselves and hear how frequently and easily we issue a quick command.

☞ There is, however, a time for commands; dangerous situations require commands. If a child is leaning out of a third floor window, a command is in order. Be sure to direct toward what you want. "Get back in!" is much more helpful and less precarious than "Don't jump!" At important times like these, a command is much more likely to work if they have not been previously overused.

Lecturing

⌂ "If I've told you once, I've told you a thousand times: Do unto others as you would have them do unto you. If you're nice to others, they will be nice to you."

⚜ "How many times do I have to tell you, if you just drop your things on the floor and don't put your jacket and lunch box in your cubby where they belong, others may trip on them and get hurt. Then what would we do?"

🍎 "You can't get good grades without studying and doing your homework. Good grades are important. You're going to need good grades to get into college. And if you don't go to college, you'll never have a good job that pays well."

Both parents and teachers have told me that they lecture because they do not know what else to do and because it feels good. Except for very young children who need brief explanations of why something is important, most of our children already know the why - we have told them - innumerable times. Children, like adults, stop listening when they already know. Have you ever seen a child's eyes glaze over while you were lecturing to her? Do you remember "teacher talk" or "parent talk" - grown-ups talking at you not to you?

The common mistaken belief is that if we tell them just one more time, they will understand *it* or remember *it* this time. In reality, they already know, understand, and remember *it*; in fact, they can usually give us the lecture quite well. The real problem is that understanding has not altered their behavior. *Telling them again does not increase their understanding and does not change their behavior.* We need to find other techniques to change attitude and behavior; we do not need to increase understanding. Yet another lecture will not net us the cooperation we seek.

☞ Brief explanations for young children and of new situations can be helpful discipline tools. Helpful explanations yield that recognizable light-bulb-turns-on look. Lectures produce a bored, blank, I've-heard-this-before look.

Reminding and Nagging

⌂ "Remember, you need to take your baseball hat and glove to practice."

🧍 "Don't forget your shoes."

🍎 "Have you started your book report? They're due on Friday."

Some of you are thinking that without your reminders nothing would get done. For young children, reminders are helpful and necessary as youngsters learn routines and necessary elements. However, we want to remind less and less as a child gets older or as the school year progresses. As well, we only want to be reminding children about things *we are still willing to own.* As one four year old, whose mother had complained of his memory lapses, explained to me, "I don't need to remember my shoes; my mommy always tells me to put them on." Out of the mouths of babes sometimes comes wisdom.

Most children need to be taught how to remember. Remembering is an acquired skill.

Notes, timers, placement of items at the back door, in the car, or under a desk, are some of the ways we can teach remembering. As well, forgetting something important can be helpful in learning to remember; let them learn this lesson young. Allowing a child to forget an important-to-her, but non-essential item or activity may at first seem cruel. It is not. Forgetting while you are young so that you see and feel the need to learn how to remember is a gift. It is also a good investment.

Assignments, test dates, and project deadlines written on a specific corner of the blackboard can greatly ease the need for reminders. A student always has access to important information simply by taking the initiative to look. Asking ourselves, "Whose job is it?" often helps alleviate reminding.

Guilt

⌂ "You know how it bothers me when you two fight with each other like this."
"When your grandparents get here, you are going to *have* to behave."
"Eat your beans for Daddy."

⚹ "Only a baby would do that."
"Pleeease be quiet."

🍎 "You *have* to be on your best behavior today. The evaluator will be here."
"Don't do this to me."
"Don't you care about the other students? They need to learn."

The person who taught us guilt is usually one of the easiest to recognize or recall. We still hear his voice even after he has left us, moved, or even died. Guilt for heinous crimes we commit may be healthy; but for daily decisions we make, guilt is not healthy. Guilt puts a child, or anyone for that matter, in a lose-lose position. For example, you decide to spend Thanksgiving dinner with your new in-laws rather than your own family. When you try to tell your mother, she replies, "You're going where for Thanksgiving? The whole family will be here. No one has ever missed a Thanksgiving. You know how important it is to me!" You lose if you go to your mother-in-law's because you will feel guilty. You also lose if you change your plans and go to your mother's because you will feel manipulated. No matter what course of action you choose, you lose. Not a comfortable feeling. The result is that we begin to distance ourselves both physically and emotionally from those who make us feel guilty and tense. When we do cooperate, it is begrudgingly. Again, this is not our goal.

Labeling and Name-Calling

⌂ "You are so clumsy."

☖ "You really do have trouble remembering things."

● "I haven't seen such poor work in years. You have terrible work habits."

Each of us has been taught, "Thou shalt not label children." Labeling is harmful to self-esteem because children believe what we adults tell them. The well-known danger is that the child begins to believe and to become the label - the self-fulfilling prophecy. Let a child know she is clumsy often enough, and she will become clumsy or clumsier, not less clumsy - which is what we were trying to accomplish.

It is frightening to realize that we can quite effectively give a negative label to a child without words - with only a look. Each of us recognizes these looks: the "you dummy" look, the "you're doing it again" look, the "I'm losing my patience, I really don't like you" look, and the "you'll never get it right" look. Sadly, we fail to recognize these on our own faces. Nor do we realize, as a general rule, the power of these forms of non-verbal communication.

There is even danger in positive labels which require living up to and maintaining. Ironically, when we tell a child how very honest he is, often within a few hours, he may lie to us. Sometimes children let us know dramatically how hard it is to live up to an image. Too often they hurt themselves physically or emotionally or learn to suppress personality and emotion in order to keep the image alive. Neither is healthy.

Comparisons

🏠 "Your brother never pulled this stuff."
"Just look at Kelly's room; isn't it nice and clean!"

👶 "Your sister never bit anyone."
"I like the way Jeremy is paying attention."

🍎 "Your sister was such a great student."
"I wish all my classes were more like my third period class."

Any of us who were compared negatively to a sibling or friend can feel our blood boil with the resentment to this day.   Intriguingly, those of us who were the recipients of positive comparisons (the good one, the smart one, the pretty one) remain uncomfortable. We fear falling off the pedestal, and we hate the resulting rivalry, bitterness, and alienation. None of us likes to be compared to someone else.

Some of you may have experienced 'proximity praise', i.e. "I like the way Jeremy is paying attention." This is a form of comparison which alienates children from one another and sets up competition, not cooperation. In both a family or classroom situation, competition increasingly is viewed and documented as destructive. Please see the discussion on praise and proximity praise beginning on page 169 in the section on Self-esteem for additional information.

A more positive side to labeling and comparing involves their usefulness in problem solving. Both, especially used together, can be most helpful in discovering how to deal with a specific child. For example, if you have a very determined child, it is helpful to mentally recognize or label this trait. Comparing how you dealt successfully or unsuccessfully with others who are very determined can help you quickly find the most effective way of dealing with this particular child. For example, pushing them did not work; but convincing them or appealing to their best interest did.   Similarly, in the classroom setting, a child who is an auditory learner benefits from a teacher who recognizes his learning strengths and weaknesses (labeling).   This teacher can then draw from her previous experience with other auditory learners in order to make learning easier for the current student.

When we use labels and comparisons *and keep them to ourselves* to help us be more effective with a child, each of us benefits. The danger occurs when we share (either purposely or unintentionally) the label or comparison with the child.

Sarcasm

"You are an accident looking for a place to happen."

"You'd forget your head if it weren't glued on."

"Of course, you can't turn it in if you don't do it."

Sarcasm is like a knife. We throw it; it cuts and does damage. Most of our children have learned some self-defense; they pull out the knife and throw it back with intent to hurt. If we did not learn sarcasm at home, we learned it from our peers during middle school or high school just to survive. Sarcasm is sometimes confused with wit, since both tend to include humor. Sarcasm is humor at the expense of someone else; wit is simply humor with words, no damage and no pain involved for anyone. Our tone, even more than our words, is always an indicator of sarcastic intent. Sarcasm is a wonderful example of the adage, "what goes around, comes around." With sarcasm, it is pain.

In conclusion, the purpose of describing the above ten disrespectful barriers to cooperation is two-fold.   First, it should be clear that these methods of addressing people do not work and, instead, create resistance, defiance, antagonism, and rebellion.   Second, it is hoped that you have identified the barriers to cooperation which you use. You may want to take a moment and think about which you use the most. Then begin to catch yourself using it. From there, you can begin to eliminate the barriers from your language - the real goal.

What then, do we want to say? How do we gain cooperation?   The answer is evident.   If violating dignity and being disrespectful create resistance, it is likely that maintaining dignity and being respectful will result in cooperation. Well, at least a much higher probability of cooperation. After all, we are talking about children and the real world.

The second ingredient of discipline, Authority, will need to be present. We need to be able to generate and maintain authority in order to be effective, to carry influence. The need for respect at a high level is constant; the requirement for authority varies in degree.

Some situations and children require a small amount of authority. At other times or with different children, a high level of authority is necessary in order to get a response. An old Chinese proverb which has some relevance here is:

> Do not use a hatchet to remove a fly from your friend's forehead.

Thus, the examples that follow always remain respectful but vary in intensity of authority. Here are six phrases, in increasing degrees of authority, which you can use and even alter to make sound more like you. We are now entering the second step of discipline: identify the problem respectfully.

4:
Respectful Language

The following are six respectful and effective ways to identify the problem and improve the odds of gaining cooperation and reduce the probability of creating resistance. It may be helpful to keep in mind that no phrase is effective in all scenarios and that each phrase may need some fine tuning to sound right to you, to become the way you feel comfortable speaking.

Guide Toward Helpfulness

How does it feel to help someone? Wonderful? At the very least, it feels good. Being able to be helpful is good for the helper; it is easy to recognize the sense of worth and accomplishment generated by helping others. Self-esteem increases as does emotional health. Offer someone an opportunity to be helpful and most will rise to the occasion. Four types of people will not: those who do not like you, in which case, you have told them exactly what not to do; those who are extremely tired, because this group is about to fall asleep and is just too tired to do anything; those whose self-esteem is so terribly low that they do not even recognize this opportunity to rebuild it; and finally, the fourth group, children who love what they are doing and strongly want to continue doing it. Otherwise, most everyone enjoys a chance to contribute to another's life. Children, especially, like the feeling of importance and 'bigness' which accompanies helping.

⌂ "IT WOULD BE HELPFUL IF you brought your dishes to the dishwasher."
"IT WOULD BE HELPFUL IF you took out the trash now."
Instead of:
"You'd forget your head if it weren't glued on. Get your dishes."
(Sarcasm, Command)
"Take out the trash!" (Command)

🧍 "IT WOULD BE HELPFUL IF you kept your hands in your pockets."
Instead of:
   "Get your hands off him!" (Command)

🍎 "IT WOULD BE HELPFUL IF you put your feet under your desk."
Instead of:
   "How many times do I have to tell you to keep your feet underneath
   your desk. Someone could get hurt!" (Lecture)

To be more direct and immediate, you may add: "Will you do that now?"

Obviously, there is no suggestion here that should you discover two children pummeling each other you say, "It would be helpful if you stopped hitting each other." "IT WOULD BE HELPFUL" does not carry nearly enough authority for such a situation. This phrasing is most useful in easy, non-threatening situations. We will discuss phrases carrying more authority later. However, both parents and teachers frequently tell me how amazed they were to discover how well this phrase works. Giving an opportunity to be helpful, rather than giving an order changes a situation dramatically. Only complying with the first opportunity is easy on our self-esteem and self-respect. Do not underestimate the capacity and potential of this phrase.

This phrase is an excellent replacement for "please." Please is a wonderful word and belongs in our communication with children. However, please does not belong in discipline because it implies a request and the option to disagree. We frequently turn ugly at this juncture. At other times, please may sound like begging, which also has no place in discipline.

Life Lessons

This phrasing teaches helpfulness and helps children feel the benefits of being helpful. Self-esteem is always higher when we choose to help.

Comfort with cooperation and responsiveness to others is also learned.

Life Messages

Bonds are strengthened when we treat children gently and considerately, as this phrasing does. Children view themselves as positive, helpful, cooperative individuals.

Children learn that they are capable.

Those who contribute to the group (family or classroom or organization) feel more welcome and attached to the group. They begin to become true members of the group. Members behave differently than non-members do. The message "I belong" is very important.

As we will discuss more in the section on Self-Esteem, this sense of belonging is a very important component of behavior, attitude, and values. Too many of our children do not feel they *belong* anywhere.

Descriptive Language[5]

This very broad method of communicating is useful in many different types of situations. By simply reminding myself to *be descriptive*, I have often managed to avoid my most common barriers to cooperation. What we are trying to accomplish is remaining purely descriptive without tossing in any accusation, guilt, command, evaluation, or threat. We simply describe the problem, the situation, or the solution. By describing what needs to be done rather than what has gone wrong, we can avoid accusations and negative comments. Some examples help make the concept clear.

⌂ For the child who arrives home and walks out of her shoes and leaves them on the kitchen floor or in the doorway.

"Shoes belong in the closet."
"You need to put your shoes in the closet."
  Instead of:
    "You forgot your shoes, again." (Blame, Put-down)

⌂ For the older child who gets up from the table without taking care of his plate.

"Your dishes go in the dishwasher when you leave the table."

"You need to put your dishes in the dishwasher when you leave the table."

Instead of:

"Pick up your dishes." (Command)

🜲 For the young child who has dropped his belongings on the hall floor.

"Your coat and lunch box belong in your cubby."

"You need to put your coat and lunch box in your cubby now."

Instead of:

"If you don't pick up your things, someone might trip on them and then what would you do? I keep telling you that you have to pick up your things." (Lecture)

🍎 For the student who (surprise, surprise) does not have a pencil.

"You need a pencil to do your work."

Instead of:

"How many times do I have to tell you, you can't do your work without a pencil? Where are your pencils? Can't you keep track of them?" (Lecture, Put down)

In each example, we tell the truth, illuminate the situation or lesson needed, and avoid barriers to cooperation with a description. We also avoid irritation and rancor.

There is debate about descriptive language and the amount of directness most helpful for individual children. For example, "You need to put your shoes in the closet" is more direct than "Shoes belong in the closet." Many experts, among them Virginia Satir in her book *Peoplemaking* and Jean Clarke in *Self-Esteem: A Family Affair*, stress the importance of direct versus indirect communication. They note that the more clear and direct, and the less ambiguous and indirect communication is, the healthier it is. There is less room for doubt, miscommunication, and mixed messages.

Jean Clarke suggests another problem with the less direct descriptive phrases such as "Shoes belong in the closet." She points out that many children will answer, "So!" Ms. Clarke prefers the "You need to put your shoes in the closet" to "Shoes belong in the closet" because the first is more direct and clearly sets up ownership of the responsibility for the shoes. A child is less likely to respond, "So!" to this type of phrasing. A good argument. On the other hand, some children are inclined to respond, "You do it!" or "NO!" to this more direct type of phrasing. These children react defensively or defiantly to the more intrusive quality of direct communication.

Because of this type of response, Faber and Mazlish emphasize, in their book, *How to Talk So Kids Will Listen & Listen So Kids Will Talk*, a desire to do as little pushing or intervening with a child as necessary to reduce this probability of defiance and obstinance. They prefer the less direct and less intervening "Shoes belong in the closet" for this reason. This, too, is good reasoning. Clearly, much depends on the child involved. Many of us recognize both types of children - those prone to replying with "So!" and those more likely to answer "No!"

Confused? Both types of descriptive language can be helpful. One, "You need to put your shoes in the closet," is more direct and healthier communication, but also more intervening and hence may cause defiance. The second, "Shoes belong in the closet," is less intervening and more likely to be responded to positively but also less direct and therefore less healthy and less honest. Generally, the choice of which to use or, in other words, how direct to be is determined by an individual child's response to them. If a child is likely to say "So!", it is more helpful to be more direct and tell her, "You need to put your shoes in the closet," or even "You need to put your shoes in the closet now." If, however, a child tends to look for a fight and power struggle, you may find that "Shoes belong in the closet" creates less resistance and is more helpful.

Both sets of authors make good points. You will need to choose whichever phrasing best suits you, or the phrasing which is more effective with each of your children or students.

Descriptive language, describing what a child needs to do, is an effective communication tool and is useful in most situations requiring a middle range of authority. It does require thought; there is no blanket statement involved.

However, with practice, describing becomes a more easily accessible format for identifying problems.

Life Lesson

Descriptive language teaches ownership of problems or mistakes and responsibility for correcting them.

I-Messages

Thomas Gordon developed another useful way of phrasing called an I-message. An I-message uses the word 'I' followed by the way you feel and the cause of this feeling. For example, "I am afraid when you climb so high." It avoids starting with the word 'you' and continuing into an accusation, "You are climbing too high." Like descriptive language, I-messages help us avoid an accusatory stance and yet encourage ownership of behavior. They allow others to know how we feel as a result of their behavior. It is critical that neither blame nor judgment be included. As well, we must be very careful not to move into the realm of guilt.

Simply starting a phrase with 'I' does not guarantee a helpful phrase. "I am angry because you're a jerk" does not qualify as an I-message. It does qualify as name-calling. These distorted I-messages are a common trap.

⌂ "I am annoyed when I have to wait for you in the morning and leave after 7:45 because I need to get to work on time."
Instead of:
"You make me late for work everyday; you just don't care." (accusation)
"I am annoyed when you make me late." (distorted I-message, includes blaming)

⌂ "I worry when you don't come home on time; I'd like you to call me when you're going to be late so I don't worry about you."
Instead of:
"Why didn't you call? I was so worried. I was sure something terrible had happened to you. If you can't call, you just won't be going out anymore!" (guilt, threat, lecture, distorted I-message)

♟ "When I find paints spilled on the table, I am irritated because I have to spend my time to clean it up later."
Instead of:
   "Jane never spills the paint when she uses it. Now, get the cloth and clean it up." (Comparison, Command)

🍎 "We are going to the museum tomorrow. I'd like us to decide what special rules we'll need to prevent any problems."
Instead of:
   "You remember what happened on our last field trip; you all behaved horribly. That is not going to happen again! There are going to be rules and you are going to follow them or there will be no more field trips." (labeling, lecture, threat)

🍎 "I am uncomfortable with the noise level in this room."
Instead of:
   "Be quiet!" (command)

It is clear that telling someone how what they do makes us feel works best with someone who cares about us. The importance of building a bond with our children or students is underscored yet again. The most common answer to an I-message is, "Oh!" or "I didn't know," followed by the appropriate corrective steps. When we routinely hear "So!" or "Who cares?!" we need to recognize the need to strengthen our relationship with this child.

Life Lessons

I-messages teach responsiveness, empathy, understanding, compassion, and sensitivity. Children learn that others have feelings, feelings sometimes caused by or contributed to by their own actions.

I-messages teach ownership of behavior, consequences, and repercussions without using blame, judgment or any of the other Barriers to Cooperation.

Give Alternatives

This type of phrase helps when a child is about to choose (or has chosen) an appropriate activity in an inappropriate manner or place, such as writing on a wall. The act of drawing is not inappropriate: the place selected is. When we only tell the child not to do something, "Don't write on that wall," she asks herself one of two questions. She may ask, "Will I quit what I want to do?" and respond, "Nah, it's fun; that's why I was doing it." Or she may ask, "Shall I do what he said or not?" and respond, "I want to do what I want to do." Most children who perceive the situation this way decide to continue doing what they want. If we add positive alternatives, we accomplish two things at once. First, we help the child focus on something other than the unwanted behavior. Second, the child still ends up with a decision to make, but a much more constructive, helpful decision: "Shall I do the first alternative or the second?" prompting "Well, which one do I like the best?" Frequently with this type of phrasing, a child passes over those first questions: "Will I quit what I want to do?" or "Shall I do what he said or not?" and addresses only the question, "Which of the positive alternatives do I want most?" We have bypassed a major struggle entirely. This is good. Here, the child's decision becomes which type of paper does she like most today? Either decision is acceptable. The child is happy because she got to make a decision, and she is still able to draw. We are happy because, at least for the moment, our walls are safe.

It is always more helpful and responsive to tell children what to do, rather than what not to do. However, in a panic, we often start with 'Don't'; should this happen to you, try to add the reason. Altering our phrasing to include descriptions and reasons helps us circumvent a quick, negative command.

⌂ "Walls are not for drawing;
    WOULD YOU RATHER draw on the plain paper
    OR on the colored paper?"
Instead of:
    "DON'T write on the wall;
    do you want to color in this notebook
    OR on this paper?"

"YOU MAY NOT ride your bike on the busy street
>   BECAUSE it's dangerous;
>   WOULD YOU RATHER ride it on the driveway
>   OR on the back porch?"

Alternatively:
>   "Streets are for cars; (or Streets are dangerous for children and bikes;)
>   WOULD YOU LIKE TO ride your tricycle on the driveway
>   OR on the sidewalk?"

"Lunches don't belong on the floor;
>   you may put it in your cubby
>   OR in your backpack."

"Use your words not your hands; say, 'I don't like that!' or 'That hurts.'"

"I am uncomfortable with rudeness;
>   rephrase and speak respectfully
>   OR take a moment and calm down and then talk to me."

Alternatively:
>   "What you said was disrespectful; disrespect will not work (or disrespect is absolutely unacceptable;)
>   DO YOU WANT TO start again respectfully,
>   OR WOULD YOU RATHER take some time to calm down before you talk to me?"

"It's important to turn in all of your homework.
>   You can turn in your Social Studies page 12 assignment by 3:00 tomorrow or go to ZAP (Zeroes Aren't Permitted program) on Wednesday."

There is one drawback to this phrasing; there can be an element of manipulation. What we have done is create a forced choice. Some salespeople use it to manipulate and trap us. Before we have said we are going to buy an item, a salesperson asks us ever so cleverly, "Do you want it in the blue or the red?" And we answer, "Well, the blue is nice." We just omitted the first decision - are we really going to buy it. We have been manipulated. On the positive side, we set up an excellent preventive dynamic by moving the area of decision-making to one that is appropriate for the child. It is important to check your intent. Are you truly offering positive alternatives or trying to slip one past a child?

> **Life Lesson**
>
> Alternatives teach children that they make some decisions; and that they still need help with others. The range of decisions increases with maturity and responsibility.

Rules, Policies, and Rights

> Authority calls for brevity. Only the weak explain themselves.
> - Haim Ginott

It was catching myself explaining to my seven year old, for the thousandth time, why he had to brush his teeth that gave the phrase "Only the weak explain themselves" a new, inspired meaning for me. One helpful answer to a child's ever-present question "Why?" is, "You tell me." Children rarely bother, and they stop asking. Most of our children know the 'whys'; we have spent years explaining to them. When it comes to discipline situations, there are several quick phrases which carry authority and are brief. Here are four in increasing order of authority.

⌂ "THE POLICY IS everyone makes her bed in the morning."

👤 "THE POLICY IS everyone who brought a jacket wears it outside to play."

🍴 "THE POLICY IS no food in the classroom except during celebrations and special projects."

Policies tend to be broader and more flexible than rules.

"THE RULE IS he who makes the mess, cleans it up."

"THE RULE IS if you play, you help pick up."

"THE RULE IS raise your hand and be called on before speaking."

The good news about rules (and policies) is that you cannot argue with a rule, unlike a person. Thus, if it is the rule, rather than the adult, which prevents a child from doing something, there tends to be much less argument, especially with young children.

> Rules and policies are most helpful when they smooth out
> operation rather than try to control behavior.

Notice that the rules and polices above address what needs to be done and help homes or classrooms run more peacefully and efficiently. Rules which address only 'Don'ts' often prove ineffective. Rules need to be stated positively as what to do, rather than negatively as what not to do. Further, negatively stated rules cannot ever cover every situation. There is always one child willing and able to conceive of something you have not thought about - spitting, washing with paint, etc. Rules can be like swords: live by them and die by them. There is danger in becoming rule-governed rather than self-disciplined. Rules are most helpful with young children where they quickly help provide structure. The reasoning behind rules needs to be explained to help children understand why a rule is in place. Our goal is not simple obedience, but understanding, agreement, and support.

In addition, a child who has helped develop and determine rules is much more likely to follow them. Changing and negotiating rules takes place at family meetings, family dinners, class meetings, or other specified times, not when the rule is about to be enforced.

Rules for Rules

☞ Keep rules positive.

> Clean up after yourself. *Instead of: Don't leave a mess.*
> Tell the truth. *Instead of: Don't lie.*

☞ Keep rules general.

> Everyone helps pick up.
> Respect yourself and others.

☞ Keep rules to a minimum.

⌂ For home:

> Speak for yourself and not for anyone else.
> Listen to others, then they will listen to you.
> Avoid put-downs; no one needs them.
> Take charge of yourself; you are responsible for you.
> Show respect; every person is important.

🍎 For classroom:

> Be here on time.
> Have everything you need to do your work.
> Respect yourself and others.

Life Lessons

Both policies and rules are the precursors to laws. There are some behaviors which are digressions and are not acceptable.

Policies and rules, like laws, inform us of the right things to do. Whether or not we abide by them is always our choice; this is self-discipline.

Structure and general guidelines can make any type of group living, home or classroom, more pleasant and efficient. Expectations are known and understood by all.

"IT IS YOUR RESPONSIBILITY TO feed the dog."

"IT IS YOUR RESPONSIBILITY TO leave gas in the car after you've used it."

"IT IS YOUR RESPONSIBILITY TO pick up the dress-up clothes when you are finished playing."

"IT IS YOUR RESPONSIBILITY TO put your cup in the trash when you're done with lunch."

"IT IS YOUR RESPONSIBILITY TO turn your work in on time."

"IT IS YOUR RESPONSIBILITY TO ask for make-up work after you have been absent."

"IT IS YOUR RESPONSIBILITY TO make sure your homework gets finished, stays safe, and is returned to me on time."

These phrases tell clearly and concisely about responsibility and ownership; they make argument difficult. They also help keep us from lecturing and giving commands and are assertive and respectful.

Life Lesson

This phrasing plainly teaches responsibility and ownership.

"YOU DO NOT HAVE THE RIGHT TO hit your brother."

"YOU DO NOT HAVE THE RIGHT TO hurt anyone in this class with your hands or your words."

"YOU DO NOT HAVE THE RIGHT TO speak disrespectfully to me or anyone."

Have you ever caught yourself saying, "I will not tolerate...!" I have only said this right after what I do not tolerate (hitting, rudeness, bad language, etc.) has occurred. Which, of course, means I have just tolerated or permitted it. (Technically, making me sound foolish.) More importantly, "I will not tolerate" is about me and my values. "You do not have the right" is about the child, correct principles, rights, and responsibility - far more important lessons. Further, "You do not have the right" carries greater authority. "Big deal" is a possible answer to "I will not tolerate." It is rarely heard in response to "You do not have the right." Clearly, this phrasing is inappropriate for small digressions. "You do not have the right to leave your bed unmade" sounds and is absurd. Keep the truth in the phrase and only use it with rights and responsibilities.

Life Lesson

This phrasing teaches the concept of rights and responsibilities; it can also teach the difference between rights and privileges.

Anger Without Destruction

Sometimes it seems as though my children lead me to the brink of disaster and then push me over the cliff. I wish I could always be calm, but I cannot. It seems I am not alone.

From the *Statistical Handbook on the American Family*, by Bruce Chadwick and Tim Heaton (1992) come the following statistics:

Percent of Parents Who Yell				
Frequency	Children Age 0 - 4		Children Age 5 - 8	
	Men	Women	Men	Women
Never	19%	17%	10%	7%
Seldom	36%	31%	33%	29%
Sometimes	40%	44%	47%	51%
Very Often	6%	7%	11%	14%

This table clearly suggests not only that there is much yelling taking place but that parental yelling increases as our children get older. For parents of children from ages 0-4, 46% of men and 51% of women report yelling at their children sometimes or very often. By the time children are 5-18 years old, these percentages of yelling increase to 58% and 65% respectively. It would be much more comforting if this trend were reversed and suggested that parents tend to improve their skills and reduce their yelling as they become more skilled, veteran parents. Unfortunately, the statistics suggest otherwise.

Rather, the table most likely reflects both increased frustration and the absence of new skills culminating in a developed habit of yelling. Most of us recognize that raising our voice is not nearly as effective a discipline tool as refraining and speaking more softly. Yet, we fail to develop skills to do so.

We do get angry with our children. We may question whether we should get mad at our children or students. The real question is *will* we get mad at them. Of course we will. We continue to let them be with us. And it is in their job description to frustrate the older generation. We also may question whether we should show our anger. The helpful question is can we not show our anger. Anger always shows through in our tone or body language. Each of us has heard someone shriek, "I am *not* mad!" Right.

Perhaps more important and disconcerting is *what* is being screamed at our children. Let us take a close look at how we can each reduce yelling and still vent our anger without destruction.

The real problem we face is that when we are angry, we many times destroy character and self-esteem. This we do not want to do. When my hands are pulsing with "Neck, neck" as I move toward the offending child, I know I need anger without destruction skills and words. I also need to carry a high degree of authority. If I am this angry, *something* has happened.

Once I witnessed one child throw scissors past another's ear just missing the second child. You can bet this got my attention. What do I want to accomplish with my discipline? I need the scissors <u>never</u> thrown again. Our words can carry a great deal more authority than we sometimes realize. Often, words coupled with appropriate touches of authority are sufficient.

What exactly are appropriate touches of authority? How can one add authority to words? Here are several suggestions.

Tips for Maintaining Authority

1. Move to the child. It is by no means necessary that every time you discipline a child with words that you must move to her. It is, however, necessary when a situation requires you to carry considerable authority; simply moving to the child lends an extraordinary amount of authority. Remember a time in high school when you committed some small infraction, and suddenly you realized that the teacher was now standing beside your desk? Remember that "oh-oh" feeling in the pit of your stomach which told you this was a bigger deal than you had expected. And this before your teacher ever said anything; she simply arrived.

2. Lower the tone of your voice from your general speaking range. Lower voices carry more authority. Higher voices weaken authority; try not to squeal in anguish or fear.

3. Lower the volume. People lean forward when we speak softly; they lean back when we yell. Yelling implies we are out of control; speaking softly indicates we are fully in control.

4. Speak slowly and clearly. This gives both of you time to think about what is being said. Speaking slowly also implies that what is being said is extra important.

5. Drop or rise to their physical level. Speak directly, face to face, on their level so that your body suggests that there will be no miscommunication. Directness, not intimidation, is the key.

6. Do try to make eye contact. However, do not get distracted by this issue. Several types of children fail to make eye contact:

• Children from many cultures are taught to show respect by looking down rather than looking at an adult speaking to them. Their body language is expressing respect as they have been taught. Many Asian, Native American,

Middle Eastern, and Hispanic children are included in this group. This is not the time to change their cultural values.

• Children who realize that what they have just done was wrong also may put their heads down and fail to make eye contact. (The last time you did something you wished you had not, what did you do with your head?) Again, their body language speaks their embarrassment and chagrin with what they have done. This, too, is a good message.

• Children who have learned to expect emotional or physical abuse may also put their heads down. They await the next blow, be it verbal or physical.

• Children who wish to express defiance, not caring, or not owning what they have done also look down - more vigorously than the first two groups who drop their heads rather than sharply looking away. This group intentionally thrusts it down to send the message, "I'm not listening; you can't get to me." For two major reasons, it is helpful not to address this missing eye contact. (Bear with me for a moment; I know this sounds strange.) First, with truly defiant children, it is virtually impossible to make them look at you. Lifting chins only results in diverted eyes. "Look at me; *look at me!*" only begins a power struggle which you will very likely lose. Plus, you have been very effectively distracted from a dangerous issue (throwing scissors) to a less important issue (eye contact). Yes, disrespect is a big issue, but not as critical as throwing scissors. Defer the concern with disrespect to be dealt with at another, more appropriate time. Limiting ourselves to one very important issue is extremely helpful. Second, eye contact is not critical. Ear contact is. Remember, they are sending the message, "I am not listening." Their body language is slightly confused and inaccurate. They are not looking; they are listening. And at present we are dealing with the thrown scissors. There is no escape. Yes, you want eye contact, and you try to make eye contact, but it is not the critical issue. Throwing the scissors is the critical issue.

7. Sometimes it is helpful to touch a child while we are speaking. Some children turn this touch into a distracting issue and scream, "Don't touch me!" It is important that as parents or teachers we recognize whom we may touch and whom we should not. All teachers, especially male teachers, must be careful about how and whom they touch. If you do choose to touch while you

speak to someone, it is called anchoring. Anchoring is a counseling technique which recognizes that the words being spoken at the time of the touch are most likely to be weighed and remembered or anchored. As we look at some ANGER WITHOUT DESTRUCTION phrases, it will become obvious that it is important to anchor at the end of the statement, not at the beginning. This delay also helps us to avoid grabbing.

In a low, firm voice, close to the child, at eye level:

⌂ "WHEN YOU throw the scissors,
    I AM scared and furious,
    BECAUSE[6] someone could get seriously hurt;
    I EXPECT you never to throw the scissors again."

If the child is very impulsive, a more appropriate phrasing is:

⌂ "WHEN YOU throw the scissors,
    I AM scared and furious,
    BECAUSE someone could get hurt;
    I EXPECT you to ask permission before you use the scissors."

🍎 "WHEN YOU continue to shout your question,
    I AM irritated,
    BECAUSE others need a turn, too;
    IT IS IMPORTANT that you let others speak.

🍎 "WHEN YOU continuously speak out in class,
    I AM frustrated,
    BECAUSE everyone's learning is disrupted;
    I EXPECT you to raise your hand and wait to be called" (or YOU DO
        NOT HAVE THE RIGHT to disrupt others' learning.)"

Depending on the situation, the last sentence can begin with I EXPECT, IT IS CRITICAL THAT, IT IS IMPORTANT THAT, YOU DO NOT HAVE THE RIGHT TO, or IT WOULD BE HELPFUL IF.

Our feelings may range from irritation to fury to scared to death. Behind each of these is usually a far more helpful and benevolent emotion, concern. All of us listen to concern more readily than we listen to anger or irritation.

When a teacher calls me about one of my children and is angry with him and tells me, "I can't get Kris to be quiet in class," I tend to turn into Mother Bear, whose job is to protect her offspring. In reaction, I perceive this teacher as weak and deal with her curtly, "What type of discipline do you have in your class that you can't keep one child quiet?" Anger begets anger. On the other hand, when a teacher calls me and is *concerned* about my child and reports, "Kris is talking a lot in class; I'm concerned that he's disturbing the other children and that he is not learning all he can," I am appreciative and recognize her for the wonderful teacher she must be. After all, she is concerned about *my* child. Rather than attacking, I respond cooperatively, "What can I do to help?" Big difference. Each teacher had the same concern and the same problem with my son. Only one of these teachers handled this situation and me helpfully. Only one do I perceive as a good guy, on my side, caring about children and about my child and me. The other teacher I feel I must push and fight. And that is exactly what happens.

These dynamics, anger giving rise to anger and concern producing concern, occur between all people. Understanding them is especially important when talking to parents about their own children and when disciplining children who are our biggest challenges, those who are emotionally and physically abused or from dysfunctional families. These children are accustomed to having people react to their mistakes with anger. We become just another person who is mad at them, and some of these grown-ups get very nasty and hurtful when angry. Children know the rules of this *Anger Game*. The child does something wrong or annoying, the grown-up gets angry, the child becomes defiant or disrespectful, the adult blows up and attacks, the child pretends not to care. Genuine concern comes as a surprise. We have altered the game format; these children know how to respond to anger; they do not know how to respond to concern. This can be helpful in breaking a cycle of behavior. Further, it is very difficult to fight with someone who is concerned with your well-being.

Each of the phrases above, as most of the situations we will need to handle, can genuinely and more helpfully use the feeling term CONCERN.

Please feel free to change any of the phrases to, "I am CONCERNED...." Use this phrase in times of your own anger, with dangerous incidents which must never be repeated, and with most troubled children and students. It is rare for this latter group to hear concern from anyone. Concern is almost always the real reason for our anger.

How will a child generally feel after a strong statement like this? Embarrassed, ashamed, bad? Is it our job to make a child feel bad? No, our job is not to *make* any child feel worse. However, it is our job to *allow* a child to feel badly about something she has done. In the above statements, the parent or teacher is never disrespectful, never belittles or shames the child. Rather, the adult descriptively shines a light on exactly what the child has done and allows the child to draw her own conclusions and feelings. We do not make the child feel bad with put-downs, negative or disrespectful comments; rather, the child makes herself feel bad when she understands and owns exactly what she has done and its results. These negative feelings about what one has chosen to do are called emotional homework. Emotional homework yields some of the most powerful, long-term behavioral changes. For this child says to herself, "That was stupid; I wish I hadn't done that. I feel awful. (Pause) Of course, I'd never have to feel this way again if I never throw the scissors again. I am *never* throwing those things again!" Now that's good thinking.

Do we need to do anything more after these words? That, of course, depends on the situation. The caution is with regard to adding a punishment which will create resentment and lead the child to stop considering what he did (in other words, what a jerk he has been) and begin to consider what you have just done to him (in other words, what a jerk you are). Punishment can stop the process of emotional homework. However, sometimes additional disciplinary action may be needed. If, for example, the scissors were thrown by a very impulsive child, the last part of the phrase needs to be changed to "I EXPECT you to only use the scissors with my permission." In this case, we could also move the scissors to a place where the child cannot reach them and will have to ask before using them. As well, place this type of child at a table or place by himself when cutting to avert temptation and unpredictability; supervise him closely. Most importantly, follow up with some form (words or action) of reconnection and affirmation - a smile, a pat, or a hug - that tells the child that it was a tough mistake, but we're still connected; he still has value. Or simply tell the child, "It was a long day and a tough lesson, but you learned it. It takes a lot of courage to learn from a mistake."

Our modeling of ANGER WITHOUT DESTRUCTION, of being respectfully assertive, is a lesson of great magnitude. Dr. Haim Ginott, in *Between Parent and Child*, stated that learning how to handle anger is the work of a lifetime. We are all pretty good with our children until we get angry. Learning how to handle anger and direct it helpfully without hurt demonstrates a very high level of maturity and development. This phrasing demonstrates one very appropriate and important way to handle anger. And not just with children!

Life Lessons

Anger frequently masks concern. Expressing the concern rather than the secondary anger is far more helpful and productive.

Children learn to do emotional homework and begin to understand that some behaviors are just not worth the aftermath of feelings which accompany them. A conscience is a most helpful item to develop.

Parents and teachers carry authority without needing force, ugliness, or disrespect. So, too, can a child.

Life Messages

I have value even when someone is very angry with me. Concern overrides anger. I am valuable.

I can learn from my mistakes. There is no problem so great I cannot handle it.

KEYS TO AUTHORITY

"Don't start what you can't finish." Always follow through with what you started. Choose your battles wisely.

Belief in yourself. Our body language (including tone of voice) reflects directly how much we believe in what we are saying and how important it is. It is critical that we are sure of what we say and how we say it. With correct principles and life lessons guiding us, we can be certain.

Concern. Concern for another's welfare and well-being is far more powerful and helpful than anger.

You may want to pause here and do the following exercise, an opportunity to "Gaining Cooperation" skills.

Gaining Cooperation Practice -
Parents

Determine your "first-thought" response; then select a response likely to generate cooperation.

1. Jason throws a fork at his younger sister.

2. Erica has left her clothes all over her room again.

3. Tom has left a huge mess after fixing a snack.

4. You need someone to close the door; you have no idea which child left it open.

5. Melissa approaches you whining.

6. When you all arrive home from the grocery store, Haley and Scott leave the car without helping unload the grocery bags.

7. The gas tank is almost empty after Jill has used your car.

8. The babysitter reports that your children misbehaved while you were gone.

Gaining Cooperation Practice -
Early Childhood Educators

Determine your "first-thought" response; then select a response likely to generate cooperation.

1. Jason throws a crayon at another student.

2. Erica has left her shoes and coat all over the classroom again.

3. You ask Tom to pick up the items he has been working with; he tells you he didn't use them last.

4. The class misbehaves while you try to talk to a parent.

5. Melissa approaches you whining.

6. Everyone but Sally and Scott are helping to pick up toys.

7. Jane refuses to wear her coat outside when it is very cold.

8. Jackie is bugging her neighbor again.

Gaining Cooperation Practice - Teachers

Determine your "first-thought" response; then select a response likely to generate cooperation.

1. Jason throws a pencil at another student.

2. Two or three students are talking while you are teaching.

3. Stacy is beginning to clown around or verbally disrupt the class.

4. The class misbehaves when a substitute teacher takes over or when they go to the restrooms.

5. Melissa approaches you disrespectfully.

6. Jane says her baby sister tore up her homework.

7. Kendra is not participating, has no book or pencil, and refuses to work on the assignment.

8. During class or in the hall, a student says, "I don't have to listen to you!"

5:
Respect as a Second Language

As you begin to alter your language, please keep in mind that this can be a very frustrating change. Most of us will be entering and using RESPECT AS A SECOND LANGUAGE. It will literally feel like a new language. Making this change requires practice and concentration. First, we have to catch ourselves using the disrespectful barriers common to us; this can be most discouraging. Many workshop participants have reported to me how very difficult this listening to ourselves process can be. Old habits die hard. People who get through this stage without hurting self-esteem are those who tell themselves, "Last week, I wasn't even aware of what I was saying. This week, I am a whole lot smarter. Next week, this will get easier and I will be better." They do not dwell on how frequently they hear disrespectful barriers; they focus on changing. They view change as a step by step process.

The next step in this change or learning process is using respectful alternatives. The actual application of this skill takes much practice. Finding respectfully assertive phrases takes time to become a more natural process, particularly when we are tired, frustrated, or angry. This is, for all practical purposes, learning a new language. The term RESPECT AS A SECOND LANGUAGE is not used lightly. It would be difficult for any of us to try to use a foreign language exclusively - even with the use of a dictionary. This is the same type of frustration and obstacle you will be facing. However, considering the benefits of addressing people the way we wish, receiving more cooperation, and beginning to break the cycle of diminishing respect, this practice and struggle are well worth the effort, and the only way to gain the return to respect we now so acutely need. No one I know has accomplished this task without real effort; thus, true commitment is critical.

☞ Choose one of the phrases which you like and which seems most natural to you and add it to your speaking. Only after you have become comfortable with the first, add a second. Trying to add three or four at once usually creates frustration. Simply trying to be more respectful is quickly forgotten.

Adding Respect to Children's Language

We have addressed making our language more respectful. The next obvious question is how we can help our children become more respectful. Teachers across the nation report that in the last two generations, both children and adults have become progressively less respectful. Yet, when I talk to parents and teachers, I hear no lessening in the strength of their value for respect. We are lacking skills. We too frequently move from nice and passive to ugly and aggressive. We miss respectful assertiveness. Part of our job as parents and as teachers is to rediscover and reteach these skills. There are four keys to adding respect to the next generation's language.

KEYS TO ADDING RESPECT TO CHILDREN'S LANGUAGE

🗝 **Be respectful**. Keep respect constantly in our own language. Always work with others from a perspective of respect. Modeling (what we practice, not what we believe) is the most powerful teaching tool we have. Respect continues to be modeled far too infrequently.

🗝 **Insist upon respect**. Insist that they approach everyone with respect. Neither accept nor overlook incidents of disrespect.

🗝 **Maintain dignity**. Avoid violating anyone's dignity during all interactions, especially disciplinary interactions.

🗝 **Teach.** Take time to teach RESPECT AS A FIRST LANGUAGE to young children. Teach RESPECT AS A SECOND LANGUAGE skills to older children. Help children with more respectful phrasing; guide them through reapproaching, interacting, and problem solving with respect. Respect is now like a second language. We have to learn it, and so must they.

6:
Gaining Cooperation Summary

Although at times we manage to manipulate or force cooperation, cooperation is not something we *take* from others. The last time you cooperated with someone, what caused you to do so? You liked the other person, you wanted to contribute, to make life easier, or to help. In short, we all cooperate *because we choose to do so.*

> **Cooperation is a *gift* from others; they choose whether**
> **or not to bestow it upon us.**

With our words, body language, and actions, we can engender resistance or cooperation; this choice is ours. Our task, then, is to help make cooperating feel more comfortable than resisting. Generally, we feel that another's lack of cooperation is their fault. We overlook our part and our ownership of the approach we use. Our approach, the words and body language we select, is a decisive factor in determining whether or not cooperation takes place. It is the only factor we control.

Respect is more than language, more than phrasing; it is a perspective from which we determine how we treat others. This perspective directs our language. The perspective we select might also be called our attitude. It is the place where respect is born and brought into true existence. Being genuine is essential.

All that has been discussed in this chapter is summed up by the words of wisdom found in the Golden Rule, a correct principle: Do unto others as you would have them do unto you. In other words, the Golden Rule asks,

"Do you choose to treat others, including children, in ways you do not wish to be treated?" The question of integrity reappears here. Are you who you want to be, who you want others to perceive you as being, who you want your children to be? Do your actions match your beliefs?

> *Believing in the Golden Rule is one thing, living it, another.*

PART III - DON'T START WHAT YOU CAN'T FINISH

7:
Discipline Strategies

We have looked at words and phrasings which help to gain cooperation. But no matter how wonderful our words are, they will not always work. And with the under three-year old set, taking action will always be a large part of discipline. We have now arrived at Step Three of Discipline: "Take the action necessary. Do what you've said you would do." The caution, DON'T START WHAT YOU CAN'T FINISH, was discussed previously. In order to avoid unending testing and loss of authority, it is necessary that once we have started discipline on a specific issue, we follow through.

Choose your battles wisely. Try not to say no arbitrarily. Take time to determine what is really important and what is not, not just right now, but for the future. Will it matter in two years, in twenty years? This judgment call, the choosing of battles, is difficult for many of us. When in doubt, talk to other parents or teachers; listen to what several people feel is important. Listen to your own little voice inside. Remember, no one knows you or your children better than you do. So when your little voice speaks, truly listen. It is usually one of your own principles speaking to you.

What, then, are some strategies we can use, actions we can take that teach life lessons and correct principles *and are effective, too?*

Disciplinary Consequences[7]

Consequences, as a disciplinary theory, continue to be misunderstood and misused. A consequence, by definition, can be anything that follows an event or an action. This could conceivably include rewards and punishments, neither of which is a form of discipline. Thus, we will use the term

DISCIPLINARY CONSEQUENCE to limit the concept of consequences to true discipline actions only. The consequences included here will always be *fair, reasonable, direct, and related.* This type of disciplinary consequence teaches ownership of not only behavior, but also of the results and effects of the behavior. Disciplinary consequences very effectively teach the fundamental principle:

> **You are responsible for what you choose to do and for what happens to you and others as a result of your decisions and actions.**

Disciplinary consequences are frequently confused with punishments and rewards. These other systems of child management use the term 'consequence' to describe punishments (check mark, name on board, loss of unrelated privilege) and rewards (marble in the jar, green card, checks). The use of the term 'consequence' in this text is strictly limited to actions which are fair, reasonable, direct, and related to a specific antecedent behavior, not simply any action taken. Making a child pay or rewarding a child are distinctly different from allowing a child to experience the related and fair or naturally occurring consequence to her behavior. Disciplinary consequences always teach a related lesson concerning the specific mistake or misbehavior; they clearly link behaviors and outcomes. Unlike punishments, they are never arbitrary or spiteful.

Early in my career, I was invited to a preschool to deal with a four year old boy whom we will call Frankie. The preschool's concern about Frankie was his continual practice of riding a tricycle into a wall in a huge gymnasium-type room. His teachers were concerned about his safety and the wall's appearance. Despite numerous measures taken to change this behavior, Frankie continued to smash into the wall.

I arrived just ahead of the time period when Frankie's group played in the large room. As expected, Frankie was the first child to get onto a tricycle. Before he started moving, I stepped in front of him and introduced myself.

"Hi, Frankie, I'm Mrs. Swift."   *He did not know me. Now it is time to tell the truth and identify the problem respectfully.*

"Frankie, your teachers tell me that you have been riding the tricycle into the wall. And they also tell me that they do not want you to do this."

No response from Frankie, except a disdainful look that says here we go again. So I proceed.

"Here's the deal, Frankie."

Now it is time to set up a disciplinary consequence by linking one behavior with its consequence and a second behavior with its consequence.

"You have a choice. You can choose to ride the tricycle and keep it away from the wall

Behavior 1, simple description, linked to:

and continue to ride the tricycle for as long as you like until snack time when they are all put away.

Consequence 1, notice I qualified "as long as you like" with "until snack time...."

Or you can choose to ride the tricycle into the wall

Behavior 2, which he already knows about, linked to:

and not get to ride the tricycle until tomorrow morning."

Consequence 2, fair and related.

It is easy to see how one can turn Consequence 1 into a reward - "If you keep the tricycle away from the wall, I'll give you a sticker." Or how Consequence 2 can be altered to punishment and control - "You can choose to ride the tricycle into the wall, and you won't get to go to story time with all the other children."

Have you ever noticed that what you say and what they hear are often two different things? Now it is time to check.

"Frankie, what did I say?"

Teens and older children may hear this as condescending; it is best used with younger children.

Frankie answers, "You said if I ride the bike into the wall, you're going to take it away."

That is not what I said; he has taken my words of discipline and turned them into a threat (barrier to cooperation) with shades of control.

"Close, but not quite. I said that you have a choice; what happens is all up to you. You can choose to ride the tricycle and keep it away from the walls, and you will be able to ride the tricycle as long as you like until they all get put away at snack time. Or you can choose to ride the tricycle into the wall and not ride the tricycle until tomorrow. What did I say?"

I tell him the truth. Once again, I link chosen behaviors with the disciplinary consequences.

Frankie mumbles, "You said if I ride the bike into the wall, I can't ride it until tomorrow."

Close enough; he is not terribly happy at this moment.

Since I have used a very appropriate discipline tool for this child and situation, and because I do carry a great deal of authority, and because I have set this disciplinary action up beautifully, one might assume that Frankie will, of course, keep the tricycle away from the wall. However, all of us who deal with real, live children realize that this is not what is going to happen. All children with self-respect and courage who face a new person and technique test us. Frankie, like other children, needs to find out if I mean what I say. The only way he can discover this is to run the tricycle into the wall. Sometimes we fail to expect this testing, this learning the lesson the hard way. Sometimes we let this testing behavior get to us and make us angry. When the child tests us, we become angry and say, "Why did you do that? Didn't I tell you not to?! How could you be so foolish, I told you I'd take that bike away!" We need to remember that it is the child who must deal with the consequences; we need to be able to stay emotionally disengaged from the child's decision. The child has made a mistake in judgment. Thus, when Frankie did decide to find out how much authority I actually carry and if I mean what I say, he ran the tricycle right into the wall and then looked for me to see what I was going to do. I was already on my way to him.

I looked at Frankie and said these very important words, "I see you made your choice (or decision)." Frankie's eyes got a little larger at this point, but he is still not terribly worried. For he, as do all children, carries with him at all times, an imaginary duffle bag full of distractors, excuses, and reasons for having done things. Frankie reaches in and says to me, "I didn't do it." I have just seen him do it, but I do not have it on video tape. It is not my job to prove he did it. In addition, this is a great distractor. If I am foolish enough to fall for it, we will spend our time arguing about whether or not he ran the trike into the wall, rather than following through with the discipline.

"You made your choice,"	*I simply restated.*
"I won't do it again," Frankie quickly replies.	*Another distractor. This is **not** the time to ask, "Just how stupid do you think I am?" Someday a teenage will tell you. Neither is it time to back down and say, "Good, ok. You've learned your lesson." This teaches children they can get away with things once, say the right phrase, and avoid discipline. As discussed previously, not following through diminishes our authority.*
"I'm glad, because tomorrow you'll be able to ride it for the whole period."	*At this point in time, Frankie decided that I might be a problem.*

He clamped on to the tricycle with both hands. It is time to take him from the tricycle. Yes, I pried his little fingers from the handlebars, left the tricycle sitting where it was, and began to carry Frankie out of the room. He is kicking, hitting, and screaming - trying to do his best to hurt me. How do I feel as I carry him past the very teachers who hired me to solve this problem? I feel just fine for several reasons. First, I have treated Frankie respectfully, fairly, and justly. I have never once violated his dignity. Second,

I could have described this scene when I was first told about Frankie, the tricycle, and the wall. He has been riding the tricycle into the wall for three weeks; he is not going to learn this lesson easily or happily. Third, I have not failed. It is not time to judge whether I have been successful. That time comes tomorrow with his second approach to the situation under the new guidelines. Fourth, I have done this child a favor. As much pain as Frankie is in presently, it is the least amount of pain he is going to experience learning this particular lesson. The earlier the lesson is learned, the lower the amount of pain - physical, emotional, social, and financial. Let us look at the long-range picture and why this is true.

The specific lesson Frankie is learning is to handle a tricycle safely and appropriately. More generally and for the long term, what I have begun to teach Frankie is a Life Lesson. Whether he will learn it forever in this first trial or whether we will only begin to build the foundation for this lesson is yet to be known. Either way, we have *invested* with our discipline. The Life Lesson is: If you choose to handle a vehicle - any vehicle - safely and appropriately, we will permit you to continue operating it. However, if you choose to handle this vehicle unsafely and inappropriately, we will wait until we think you are more ready before we allow you to use the vehicle again. You do not have the right to hurt yourself, others, or objects with carelessness or recklessness. Frankie can learn or begin to learn this concept at the tricycle level reasonably inexpensively. Or he may end up learning it at the car level at the cost of another person's life - a far greater price, with far more pain. I have given this child a gift, the beginnings, and perhaps even the completion, of a very important life lesson. Considering some of the other options for learning this lesson, his pain, as great as it is to him right now, is minimal compared to what it might have been. Not a bad gift. Of course, Frankie does not see this, nor is he going to thank me now. Nor will he think of me on the day he is driving carefully through a school zone and consequently manages to avoid hitting a child who dashes into his path. But I have contributed to his life, his self-discipline, and his well-being. So I need to understand the worth of what I have done. I feel good while I carry this very upset child out of the room - very good.

Evaluation of this disciplinary procedure comes the next morning when he again heads straight for the tricycles. It is here where Frankie altered his thought process and thus his behavior. Each morning prior to my intervention, Frankie asked himself this question, "Do I want to ride the bike into the wall or not?" The answer was, "Yes, I love smashing into it!" Today his thought process is more helpful, "Do I want to ride the bike or not? Yes, I love the bike! Of course, I have to keep it away from the stupid wall in order to be able to ride it." So be it. After disciplinary consequences, his question changes from the behavior level to the consequence level. Rather than choosing between behaviors (to crash or not), Frankie chooses between consequences (to ride or not). One small step for Frankie, one giant step for self-discipline.

Here are some additional examples of disciplinary consequences.

"YOU HAVE A CHOICE;
YOU CAN CHOOSE to play nicely (cooperatively) <u>AND</u> continue playing with your friends, or
YOU CAN CHOOSE to continue bothering them <u>AND</u> have to play by yourself."

"YOU CAN DECIDE to pick up your toys <u>AND</u> you will own them, or
YOU CAN DECIDE to leave them, <u>AND</u> I will pick them up and keep them until Friday."
Better still:
"You can pick up your toys, <u>AND</u> you've done your chore; or you can leave them, and I will pick them up, <u>AND</u> you will owe me a chore. Your choice of chores will be gathering up laundry or cleaning up after supper."

"YOU CAN CHOOSE to keep your hands to yourself <u>AND</u> continue working at this table, or
YOU CAN CHOOSE to put your hands on other people <u>AND</u> move to another table."

"YOU CAN redo this paper <u>AND</u> raise your grade, or
YOU CAN leave it as it is <u>AND</u> earn the failing grade on it."

☞ Paint a picture of *linked* actions and consequences with your
words. Note the <u>AND</u> in each clause. Take a child down both
complete paths. Each time the first choice links one behavior to its
consequence, and the second choice connects the alternative
behavior with its consequence. In this way, we help children
choose between desired consequences (passing or failing) rather
than between desired behaviors (doing more work or doing no
work). This helps a child perceive and be more comfortable with
the reasons behind the more appropriate choice.

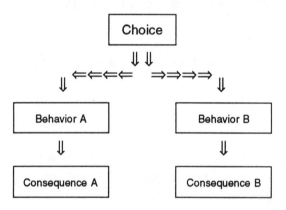

Another helpful phrasing for disciplinary consequences involves a WHEN
YOU, THEN YOU sequence.

🏠 "WHEN YOU pick up your room,
(THEN) YOU may read (leave, go out and play, watch television, go on
to your next activity, do what you want)."

🧒 "WHEN YOU pick up your lunch box,
(THEN) YOU may play with the blocks."

🍎 "WHEN YOU have finished your class work,
(THEN) YOU may start your homework (read your book, play the math
games)."

Unless a child is tired or ill, he cannot handle doing *nothing* for very long.
Keep in mind, holding you up or working against you as you get agitated is

doing *something*. If you can remain detached, your child will have nothing to do. This "when you have completed the necessary task(s), then you can go on to your fun activities" is a wonderful life-long lesson (work first, play after) as well as an effective tool for the present. It is *not* the phrasing of choice when *you* are in a hurry.

☞ Consequences are most effective when they are immediate and inevitable, not harsh.

Trying to find and use the biggest consequence often backfires. When my children were pre-schoolers, I became irritated with them because their room was yet again a mess. Knowing that the once-a-year, very popular, big event Santa Claus parade was happening later that morning, I pronounced that when their room was cleaned up, we could go to the Santa Claus parade. I knew they very much wanted to go, but I overlooked two very important factors. First, they were so excited about the parade that it was virtually impossible for them to stay on task. Second, only a mean, evil, wicked mother would not take her children to this wonderful event. Good mothers take their little Santa Claus-believing children to the Santa Claus parade. It was not acceptable to me to not take them, especially for not having picked up their room well enough. Consequences must be fair, not harsh to be most effective and helpful. In addition, consequences must be tolerable to the parent. Never set up something you are uncomfortable following through with, because your bluff will be called.

☞ When you catch yourself asking what can I use to get this child to do what I want, understand that you have crossed over into manipulation, rewards, or punishment.

☞ Consequences easily become threats ("IF YOU ..., I WILL...."); when imposed in anger, these aim to make the child pay, not learn.

☞ Forcing or inventing consequences usually fails and frequently involves punishment and control. ("You can choose to pick up your toys or to get a spanking.")

☞ As wonderful a tool as disciplinary consequences are, no tool is appropriate in every situation. Other tools will be needed as well.

☞ As children age, they can be involved in establishing consequences; they are then more likely to cooperate and to make more appropriate decisions.

Life Lessons

Consequences help children learn to think ahead to effects and repercussions of behaviors. They teach children to own both behaviors and results. Children learn to make decisions based on consequences or outcomes rather than behaviors.

Children learn to work or finish important tasks before play.

Children learn that when they behave appropriately, responsibly, and maturely, freedom and privileges increase. They move and grow into their lives.

Direct to Remedy, Amends, or Contribution

When a child makes a mess, breaks or loses something belonging to another, or hurts someone, it is important that we help him understand the need for repair, restoration, or restitution. Our focus too often is on what went wrong rather than on what needs to be done to fix it.

⌂ "The milk is spilled. Do you know where the dish cloth is?"

⌂ "I'm glad you had a good time. The dress-up clothes are all over the floor. Now you need to put them back in their box. Will you start with the ones on your bed or those on the floor?"

⌂ "When you use my car, you do not have the right to use up all the gas. I need at least enough gas to get to work."

⌂ "Did you enjoy lunch? Me, too. Now it's time for us to clear the table."

☗ "Oops, the paint spilled on the floor. The sponges are back by the sink."

☗ "You sat on his crayon. Can you find him another green one in the box?"

🍎 "Your test tube is broken; you will need to bring money for a replacement tomorrow."

🍎 To the student who has ruined another's pen:
"Do you have an extra pen in your desk?"

Life Lesson

Here is a wonderful opportunity to help children learn the concept: Whenever you undo (harm, break, damage) anything or make something wrong (lose, disturb, alter), it is your responsibility to make it right again (fix, replace).

Occasionally we are unable to make true amends - as when an antique is broken or a personal memento is lost. This, too, can be an important life lesson. While playing with a ball in the living room (against house rules), my son broke one of three graduated glass candle holders which had been a wedding gift. He very willingly cleaned up the glass and offered to buy me a new one. The set, of course, was not to be found anywhere. Replacement was impossible. Saddened though he was, he learned that making it right is not always possible. It is far less painful, both emotionally and financially, to learn this with a ball and a glass candle holder than with a car and a child. When you kill a person by driving carelessly, you cannot replace him or make amends - *no matter how badly you may wish.* This is one of life's harshest lessons: best to learn it early and inexpensively.

We begin teaching children to contribute by maintaining themselves and taking care of their own needs and business, such as getting dressed and picking up their own toys. As children get older, we add that it is also their responsibility to contribute to the family. By teaching our children how to do all household chores, we are able to send them off to college or work with adequate survival skills. We want it to be a luxury to bring home laundry, not a necessity. We do them a disservice by not helping them learn. After all, do you want your own child to marry someone who neither knows how to do chores nor expects to do them?

We also start teaching them to contribute to larger arenas of their lives. As noted previously, no matter what group we belong to, family, classroom, school, church, organization, nation, planet, we need to contribute to its general welfare and maintenance. No group can afford parasites. No one has the right to be a long-term or permanent parasite; short periods of no contribution in times of great duress and need are, of course, acceptable.

Taking care of only our own life and our own problems is not enough. Each of us finds himself in need of help and contribution from others at various times. This is perhaps the best use of a *credit system*. Healthy marriages and good relationships of every kind build a surplus of contributions; one never knows when the tables may turn and the resources be needed. We need to have enough resources.

⌂ "Our whole house needs cleaning today. Would you rather vacuum the carpets or mop the kitchen floor?" If they ask why they have to do it, *tell them*, briefly.

♣ "It's time to wipe off all of the tables."

🍎 "After all of the cutting we've done for this project, we need to pick up all the scraps on the floor."

🍎 "It's time to clean up the lab."

Life Lesson

Contributing teaches a truth: people need people.

Life Message

There is no problem so great I cannot deal with it or handle it.

Problem? Think!

When children face problems, we have an opportunity to build self-esteem and confidence and send the message, "I can think for myself." Too often, we move in with our own solutions and generate resistance or sabotage or helplessness. It is critical that we let children practice thinking and problem solving skills on *child-size* problems so that their skills have a chance to grow and develop with their problems, which seem only to get larger as we age. Further, children become comfortable with the fact that problems are part of every-day life and relationships; the key is to stay calm and work together to find a plan that just might work for everyone.

⌂ "You both want the same toy (as you take possession of the offending toy); this is a problem. What are some ways to handle this situation?" *(Until you take possession, no one will listen.)*

⌂ "Both of you feel it is your turn to ride in the front seat. Don't try to convince me; work it out between you. You have 15 seconds, or I will solve it; my solution is for you both to be in the back."

⌂ "You each want to watch different TV shows (as you turn off the television and take possession of the remote control). How can you two solve this?"

⌂ "You both need the car; when you've worked out a solution, come get the keys."

⌂ "Here is a list of the chores the three of you need to do by noon. You determine how you will divide them, and let me know who is responsible for what before you begin."

♟ "You both want the same chair. What can you think of to do about it?"

♟ "You both need the computer; let's work out a solution that is agreeable to both of you."

🍎 "You both want to sharpen your pencil. The rule is only one person at the pencil sharpener at a time. Decide who should stay and use the sharpener and who needs to return to her desk. You have 10 seconds or both of you will have to sit down."

🍎 "You both want the same report topic; everyone needs to have a different topic. You have until tomorrow morning to work this out. I'll be here right after school if you want some help."

☞ Help guide them through alternatives and problem solving until you find a solution agreeable to the parties involved.

☞ Young children or children who have *not* learned or practiced problem-solving skills need to be taught these skills by modeling or walking through problems appropriately **before they are left on their own to solve problems.** Abandoning children by saying, "It's your problem, you solve it," may lengthen the learning process or allow unhealthy practices (manipulation, coercion) to develop.

Life Lessons

When we have a problem, we need to think, work together, and come up with a plan, which is mutually acceptable to all involved.

Children learn that helplessness is not acceptable or necessary.

Problems will always be with us. Our job is to take care of it as efficiently and cheerfully as possible.

Life Messages

Children who have conquered problems build the belief system: I can think for myself and I can solve problems.

They are also immunized against discouragement and even suicide. These children understand that life is filled with problems, but these can all be worked through, by oneself or with help from others.

Use Humor

Humor is a wonderful way to change moods and slide through troubled times. In our family, humor is the lubricant which helps us keep functioning; without it, we truly would be lost and life would be uglier. When I am too tired to get into *real discipline*, I often reach for humor. Children almost always respond positively. It is important to keep the humor within the child's level; it is easy to go over a child's head. Humor is aided by our bond; I would only ask a child who feels absolutely safe from physical harm from me if he wants to continue in his present life-form. Not having previously established this sense of trust and safety would prevent me from using humor of this nature.

The most frequently asked question I receive about using humor is, "How do you find it?" I truly do not know. Drawing upon shared experiences and stories can help. I do know that it is worth working on and developing. Here are some examples.

To the child who gives you an evil look:
⌂ "That look is ugly, but it's not up to your regular standard. I know you can do better." (It is very hard to make ugly faces when you are laughing.)

Sometimes by the end of the day, after struggling to get to bed, none of us feels very loving; yet I hate to miss this nightly opportunity.
⌂ "The Mommy Handbook says we have to kiss goodnight, but it doesn't say we have to enjoy it." (I confess, I frequently refer to this non-existent, product of my imagination.)

👶 Tickle a child into changing his mood and his mind.

🍎 When two students are talking or one is clowning around, walk near them and hold up a small stop sign; you won't need to say anything.

☞ <u>Always</u> avoid sarcasm, derision, mockery, belittling, and ridicule - anything which makes fun of a child. Using humor consists of fun with them, not fun at their expense.

> **Life Lesson**
>
> Life and people do not always do as we would wish; a sense of humor helps our mood, our attitude, our health.

Take Action - Physical Discipline

For a time, in my seminars, I would say tongue-in-cheek, "Some of you are saying to yourselves - physical stuff *finally!*" I no longer say this because physical abuse has risen to such a disturbing level. Our generation, as parents, caregivers, and teachers, needs to wipe out physical abuse. In part, this means we need to abandon striking, slapping, shaking, shoving, grabbing, biting, spanking, in short, hurting children in any way. Physically hurting children is an extreme form of punishment which we have for years known creates resentment and backlash. It is remarkably short lived, produces immunity, stops working, and destroys relationships. Furthermore, it is *not effective.* If it were effective, one would not have to keep doing it, nor keep increasing the severity. Step by step, increment by increment, a parent moves toward abuse. And keep in mind that many victims of physical abuse become adult perpetrators and perpetuators.

Hitting also teaches appalling lessons and flawed principles. Too many people have learned to operate their lives on flawed, potentially harmful principles that say: 1) we solve problems with aggression and pain and power, 2) if someone does something, however minor, that you do not like, you do have the right to hit or hurt that person, and 3) aggression and violence are respectable ways of solving problems. We need to be teaching our children the correct principles in the following life lessons.

> **Life Lessons**
>
> You do not have the right to hurt anyone even if you do not like them or do not approve of what they are doing (except in self defense, defense of others, illegal actions, extreme situations).
>
> Actions speak loudly. Taking disciplinary action sends the message that we mean business. We can mean business without being mean.

What do we mean by physical discipline? The adult gets up and takes action and is physical in response, not just verbal. Although this type of technique works with all ages of children, it is especially helpful with young children (1-7 years) and tired children. Some examples follow.

- Walk a child to her bedroom, to her chore, to a destination.

- Take several children to bed by 'train' - place hands on the waist of the person in front of you and travel locomotion style.

- Carry a child piggy-back to the bath tub.

- Put the hockey stick left out *again* into the shed.

- Remove yourself from whining or disrespect.

- Remove a child to her bedroom or outside or another area of the house.

- Remove an 'offending' toy.

- Sit a squirmy, distracted, or aggressive child on your lap at circle time.

- Take the hand of a child who runs when she needs to be walking. (Have her verbally commit to walking all the way to the play area before you release her. Give only one opportunity to get it right.)

- Involve a child in songs by helping him with hand motions.

- Put objects which seem to lead to trouble in the cupboard.

- Stand by the bathroom door when a 'creative child' washes her hands or on an I-am-finding-all-kinds-of-trouble day.

- Walk and teach near a student or group not attending well. Walk throughout your class frequently.

- Begin walking a student to the gym.

🍎 Help walk a child away from trouble.

🍎 Gently put your hand on a student's shoulder to quiet him down or to bring back focus. Alternatively, lightly tap his desk or paper.

🍎 Meet your class as they return from gym or recess.

🍎 Stand by your door or in the hall during most passing periods. This action significantly changes hall behavior in a school where teachers do this consistently.

Outsmart Them

Outsmarting children is difficult but not impossible. It is also one of my favorite strategies. Included in the concept of outsmart them is *do no harm and take no advantage*. Manipulation is not involved. This strategy simply means outthink a problem or situation.

🏠 As a bedtime ritual, read to your children IN THEIR OWN beds, AFTER bath, toilet, and tooth brushing. BRING one drink. For a time, we read to our children on the couch and then had to get them to their beds; this change of venue tended to unsettle them and make them ready to play again. Children settle down and settle in when reading; take advantage of this situation (not the child) by reading to them where they can fall asleep. Sometimes a child's second wind can last longer than ours.

🏠 'No' is the answer to any question asked or any request made when you are on the phone.

🏠 Buy an alarm clock; let *it* wake up your child.

🏠 Use a timer to tell them when to take turns, when to get out of the bath, when to come in from the backyard. A child can argue with you, but there is no arguing with a clock. (There is tampering with it, though. Sometimes to complete this outsmart them arrangement, the clock must be placed out of reach, or you will need to set the kitchen timer as well.)

⌂ Send them outside! I mean *allow* them to play outside.

⌂ Call a friend. Call a friend for each of them.

⌂ Choose your neighborhood wisely, when possible.

⌂ For fighting: Place them on a couch or in two separate chairs and tell them they can get up when they give each other mutual permission.[8] Explain mutual permission.

⌂ When things get noisy, ugly, or out of control, call for Absolute Silence for five minutes. Or play the see-who-can-be-quiet-the-longest-game.

⌂ Play a child's tape in the car or at sleep time. Use coordinating tapes and books. To paraphrase, you can lead a child to bed but you cannot make him sleep. Give the mind something to do so the body can be quiet.

⌂ On long trips, plan stops to eat, outside if possible, to run and get rid of built-up steam. Take along new or special used-only-in-the-car toys and activity books. Check your local children's book store for activity ideas.

⌂ Have Santa or his elf helper visit (unseen, of course,) early in December and bring Christmas crafts, puzzles, books, and other fun things to do. It is awfully hard to wait for that one big night. Do the same for other long awaited, eagerly anticipated occasions such as Halloween and birthdays.

⌂ Give transitional warnings. These are frequently suggested for young children; they also prove most helpful with older children, even teens.
> "We need to leave the park in five minutes; go and do whatever you most want to do; otherwise, you won't have time to do what's most important to you."
> "At noon, the (rented) video game has to go back to the store."
> "Your room needs to be finished before we leave in ten minutes."

Early childhood educators incorporate the 'outsmart them' concept as well as any group I have ever met:

🧍 Allow children to bring a cuddly toy from home for nap time.

🧍 Have lots of activities, as well as space for quiet times.

🧍 Give them several opportunities to play outside or do gross motor activities.

🧍 Sing with them when you move from one room to another or when you get caught and need to wait in line.

🧍 Add hand motions and finger play to songs, rhymes, and stories.

🍎 'No' is the answer to any request made while you are talking to another student, teacher, or parent.

🍎 Questions which interrupt inappropriately are not answered.

🍎 When a student is not paying attention, move to the student, make eye-contact, and ask a question looking directly at this student. At the very end of the question, slide your eyes to the student behind or beside the one not attending, and using the second student's name direct the question to him. The student not paying attention is grateful for at least twenty minutes, and you have lost no valuable teaching time.

Life Lesson

Gentleness, respect, consideration, and thinking are healthy, acceptable methods of influencing others; manipulation is not.

Determine What Child Needs[9]

Interestingly, parents and teachers rarely consider this action a disciplinary one. Many times, meeting a child's needs will avert or short circuit a problem quickly and easily. No one ever said we had to make child-rearing more difficult than it already is. This technique is frequently used with babies and toddlers; it can also be helpful with older children. What types of needs can we meet? Bodily comfort for young children - hunger, discomfort, wetness, position change, temperature adjustment, boredom, over-stimulation, and fatigue. There are also emotional needs such as attention, affection, affirmation, emotional safety, and understanding. As well, there are needs stemming from frustration and thwarted efforts which require problem solving help. Providing developmentally appropriate activities and materials also meets needs.

⌂ Give attention, even in small amounts, throughout the day. Leave extra time at the end of the day, at reunion times, and at bed time. Schedule regular times to be together.

⌂ Help with big jobs such as cleaning a bedroom. It is difficult for children to stay with a task which seems overwhelming. Working with them helps. I only work as long as they are working; I explain I am here to help, not to perform single-handedly.

⌂ Be sensitive and perceptive! Listen and watch.

⌂ Provide a small climbing apparatus inside or allow them to play with sofa pillows and cushions.

⌂ Select one floor level cupboard and place all of your plasticware in it; allow access to small children.

⌂ Teach your children to say, "I need a hug," when they need some attention. Stop what you are doing and hug them when they ask.

⌂ Be affirming; encourage and teach others to be affirming.

⌂ Help with problem solving.

⌂ Be available at times of crisis and major need.

⚐ Use developmentally appropriate practices (DAP).

⚐ Provide water and sand play, gross and fine motor activities, quiet times, social times, and rest periods.

♠ Help direct the peg into the hole. (Help with problems.)

♠ Be sensitive and perceptive! Listen and watch. Be affirming; encourage and teach others to be, as well. Help with problem solving. Be available at times of crisis, major need.

🍎 Address various styles of learning; incorporate all into your teaching and activities.

🍎 Allow children to go to recess; they need the break.

🍎 Teach students non-irritating ways to seek your attention; teach them appropriate and inappropriate times to approach you.

🍎 Include activities with group discussions and movement throughout the day. For all students, most especially middle school or junior high students, provide learning opportunities which involve group work. Direct what they talk about instead of trying to keep them quiet.

🍎 Be sensitive and perceptive! Listen and watch. Be affirming; encourage and teach others to be, as well. Help with problem solving. Be available at times of crisis and major need.

Life Lesson

You do not have the right to be disrespectful, hurtful, or ugly anytime. Even when you are frustrated or angry, you still need to find ways through or around obstacles. Others may even be willing to help you.

Life Message

I am valuable and likeable and important.

Trade or Substitute[9]

This, too, is a common discipline tool with young children, yet it can be helpful with older children.   This tactic simply involves substituting an appropriate item or activity for an inappropriate one.

⌂ When the baby wants to "make rain" over the kitchen floor with his sipper cup of juice, substitute water for the juice and the bath tub or the back yard for the kitchen.

⌂ When a child is frustrated because he wants to take a good spoon out to dig in the sand, give him an old spoon, a trowel, or a plastic shovel.

⌂ When your eleventh grader wants to go into the city or to a basketball game in another town, let her use the more reliable family car for the evening rather than the older one she usually drives.

⌂ Instead of quitting work, find a different, better job.

⚹ When the child wants to go down the slide head first, remind him to go feet first with your words or a gentle physical position change.

🍎 Offer all of your students, including the class clown, the opportunity to act out a scene from their books rather than write a book report.

Life Lesson

We do not always get exactly what we want; but if we can be flexible, we end up with more options and more pleasure in life.

Limit the Environment Rather than the Child[9]

Some of you are thinking, my child will learn not to touch the items on the coffee table. Others of you are thinking, my child will never learn not to touch (at least not for years). It is just not worth my constant vigilance. Some of you are blessed with both types of children.

Children are remarkably different. What works best with one does not necessarily work well with another. Parents, too, differ in values and expectations. What works best for one parent may not work well for or even be acceptable to another parent.

When limiting the environment is acceptable to you, it becomes a discipline tool which can ease life rather than make it more difficult. Especially when children are young, postponing a life lesson and making your life easier is a valid and helpful option - at times. When a child is young, a lesson (not touching breakables) may take repeated disciplinary action to learn. If, on the other hand, a parent waits a month, six months, a year, the lesson may be easily, quickly, and relatively painlessly learned. *Timing in this case is the parent's choice.* Limiting the environment, rather than the child, is one method of accomplishing this.

- Always child proof for danger. No one, no matter how careful, is vigilant every second, and seconds are all it takes.

- Child proof for precious items and ease of life. Sometimes when a cherished item is broken, it is difficult to remember that people are more important than things. Some items are themselves a hazard to young children. We had a beautiful glass table which we did not use for several years because it was exactly the wrong height for wobbly toddlers.

- Remove temptation. Children are about as good with temptation as we adults are - in other words, not very. Out of sight frequently can be out of mind and out of trouble. Chocolate candies left on the counter beg to be eaten. A ponytail just within reach says, "pull me, pull me." And a car left running, implores "drive me, just take one little spin around the block!"

- Fencing in our own backyard eased my life more than almost anything else ever did.

- Invite a playmate to come play.

- Go to a park; life is always better at the park.

- Keep scissors in a cupboard or closet.

♣ Watch when they paint; paints talk to young children - "Taste me; try me on your clothes or body or in your hair; I would look great on your buddy; I would look great on the hamster."

🍎 Create an 'office' in your classroom where students may go to work quietly and without distraction. Only purposeful workers go to this office.

🍎 Take possession of toys and small objects which come out to play during work time. Return at the end of day. If they come to play again, return at the end of the week, six-weeks, or semester, or request that a parent come to claim them.

🍎 Move your desk. Move their desk closer to you or away from other students. Separate the talkers.

Life Lessons

Temptation is very difficult to resist. Sometimes it is helpful to remove it from sight or access.

Simply altering our environment can make life easier and smoother.

Redirect

This strategy involves diverting or redirecting children. Redirection can take place as problems arise or to prevent their occurrence. Redirection is the single most common form of discipline for under three's. It generally is a truly gentle and subtle form of discipline.

⌂ When you see frustration start to build, help a child change to a less upsetting activity. For example, when a child is becoming annoyed with the block tower that keeps falling, suggest: "Let's look at your books for a while."

⌂ To the child getting louder at the table: "Use your inside voice."

To the child about to hit in anger: "Use your words, not your hands." Make sure you teach what types of words to use.

When a group of children playing with dolls start to get too noisy, begin to softly sing a lullaby. They cannot resist helping to put the 'babies' to sleep.

When a child is standing and waiting for a favorite activity, suggest: "It's not your turn to paint yet. Would you like to play with the clay or the blocks?"

"Tackle football is not allowed. You may play touch football though."

When a student who is supposed to be working is off in space, walk by and point to the place on his paper where he needs to resume working.

Life Lessons

When a door is shut, frequently a window opens.

A little bit of flexibility goes a long way.

Empower Yourself

As the saying goes, he who hesitates is lost. Life is filled with incidents where we simply do not know what is the best thing to do. Many of these predicaments occur when we need to discipline a child. Whether we lack confidence, skills, or vision, we end up feeling powerless or helpless, in short, victimized. When we feel helpless, we are most likely to turn ugly and return to our worst old habits or to stop trying altogether. Neither of these is helpful. Just as we never want a child to feel helpless, so we wish to empower ourselves with the knowledge, "I can think and do for myself. I am capable." It is, however, unrealistic to expect always to know what to do as a parent or a teacher. A truly critical concept for each of us is the realization that it is the wise person who *STOPS AND THINKS* when in doubt or bewilderment. This can be accomplished in two ways. First, when we are faced with a new situation, it is perfectly prudent and excellent modeling to tell a child: "I am not sure how I want to handle this, but as soon as I decide, I'll get back to you. Until that time, no one plays with the paints."

Take time to collect your thoughts, talk to your spouse, or check a resource. The child, having read your irritation, exasperation, or anger, spends time stewing over what she has done and what will happen. Clearly, this has limited usefulness with very young children who generally cannot remember what they did five minutes ago; children under three require a more immediate response.

Children often repeat misbehavior. This gives us a warning. The second way to empower ourselves involves repeated behavior. Fore-warned can be fore-armed. It allows us to determine how we will deal with a child the next time the behavior returns. When confronted with a repeated misbehavior, it is most beneficial to take a quiet period (during naps, at bedtime, after school, while driving) and simply think about what is bothering us the most. Then determine what lesson needs to be learned and how we can best teach it. By developing a plan, we avoid becoming trapped as helpless victims and slowly going crazy. The next time we are confronted by the repeated behavior, we are ready with what we want to say and what we need to do. This works well when a general feeling of malaise is present. What is helpful is discovering exactly what is bothering us and what we want to do to change it. Again, merely having a plan decreases stress. In short, we need to be prepared.

In the classroom, it is sometimes helpful to put off discipline until a natural or scheduled break in the lesson or day occurs. Problem solving sometimes needs to wait because it requires extra time. However, delaying discipline is a technique which can be abused. When possible, discipline is more helpful the closer it occurs to the incident. This strategy is for new and innovative behavior by a child which throws off or surprises the parent or teacher.

Life Lessons

No one knows everything. And we are not supposed to!

When in doubt, wise men and women stop and think before taking action. Take *NO ACTION* when angry.

Being prepared is good for more than scouts; it is a life skill.

Enhance Self-esteem

There are numerous important reasons for building self-esteem apart from discipline. However, building self-esteem is also a powerful discipline technique. There is a direct relationship between self-esteem and discipline. Children with low self-esteem have issues to deal with, for example: proving themselves, being the best, always looking good to others, manipulating others, obtaining and using power. They are also more difficult to discipline. A child with high self-esteem may need only a glance, a gesture, or a quick word to return to appropriate behavior; children with low self-esteem typically require more intervention. To summarize:

The greater the value for self,
> the lower the probability of misbehavior (fewer digressions),
> the higher the probability of cooperation (easier discipline), and
> the greater the frequency of self-discipline (no need for outside intervention).

Life is simpler when self-esteem is solid and high. There is age old wisdom in the adage "An ounce of prevention is worth a pound of cure." Prevention is a wonderful investment. By building and affirming self-esteem, we make discipline incidents and procedures easier, and we prevent a remarkable number of incidents all together. We reduce both the frequency and intensity of discipline. What a tremendous bonus.

Neither parents nor teachers can afford to overlook the importance of their relationship with children. Each of us remembers a high school teacher we liked and one we did not. Not only did we learn more from the one we liked (kids don't learn from people they don't like), but we also behaved much better for the teacher we liked (kids don't behave for people they don't like). Healthy families work together; so do healthy classrooms. We do not need to be best friends with our children and students. We do, however, need to be affirming, fair, and respectful. When strong relational bonds are built, children more easily and more frequently choose to work with us. When bonds are weak, or when children do not like us, they choose to work against us and drive us nuts for the fun of it. The older the child, the more sophisticated and capable he is at making life together difficult. The less emotionally healthy, the greater the difference between how a child behaves for an adult she likes or with whom she has a strong bond and one she does not like and with whom she does not have a relationship. Good, strong bonds are an essential ingredient of discipline. Affirming self-esteem is one key to building bonds; the second key is respectful treatment. How much a child perceives we value and like her contributes to the strength of our bond. How we treat a child both during, and outside of, discipline determines the strength of our bond.

The bond between adult and child is a critical ingredient of discipline with children of all ages. As children enter the teen years, the bond reveals its importance. At the beginning of their middle school years, I asked each of my children how many of their friends liked their parents. Each answered that most of them liked their parents. When I inquired again at the end of their middle school years, the answer had changed to only half. When the bond is weak, when children do not really like a parent or a teacher, it becomes very difficult to discipline effectively. A healthy, strong bond eases the frequency and degree of discipline. Taking time and effort to build bonds is a valuable investment. It can make a tremendous positive impact in discipline.

During the teen years, a strong bond can be the difference between "living is easy" and "life is hell." Apart from all of the discipline that you have given to your child up to her teen years, no factor is more important nor contributes more to the ease of dealing with a teen than a strong positive bond. Child-rearing is, or at least can be, about relationship building. If our children do not learn to forge healthy relationships in their youth, when and how will they master this important life skill?

Life Lessons

Life is easier when we are nice, respectful and affirming. Bonds are built, and people are more likely to work with rather than against us.

Other people are valuable. Other people are likeable, and can be depended upon and trusted.

Life Message

I am valuable. I am likeable.

8:
Problem Solving

The best way out of a problem is through it. - Unknown

Problem solving is a wonderful discipline tool used when we sense a child is choosing to work against us, or at the very least is not choosing to work with us. It is also extremely helpful in cases of repeated misbehavior. Problem solving with children teaches children important problem solving skills and life-long lessons. There are six steps to problem solving.

Define the Problem

It is at this first step into problem solving that we often fail to sufficiently engage the child. It is crucial that we describe the problem we see from *both* our and the child's viewpoints; when we only include our viewpoint, the child has no reason to enter into problem solving. Further, he has reason - we want to change him and get what we want - *not* to enter problem solving. Always include the child's vested interest or reason for wanting a particular problem solved. Here are some examples:

 "I am wondering if you feel not getting along with your brother and having him bug you so much is a problem?"
Instead of:
"I'm tired of you and your brother fighting all of the time."

⌂   "I don't like having to remind you about your chores, and I bet you're
tired of my nagging. Let's see if we can find a way to settle these
issues of chores and nagging."
Instead of:
"You never want to do your chores. Let's find a way to work this
out."

🏃   "Sometimes you need a specific color and someone else is using it; we
need to look for some ways to help everyone get the crayon he
wants as quickly as possible."
Instead of:
"You are going to have to find a way to share these crayons."

🍎   "The noise level in here is too high, and you all need to talk to your table
partners to finish your projects. How can we solve this?"
Instead of:
"We have to do something about the noise level in here!"

Take time to listen to the child's point of view and to her feelings about
the situation. Her point of view is as important and valid as the adult's; not
taking enough time to listen can result in the child's leaving or sabotaging the
process or in working on the wrong problem. Paradigm shift as a
communication tool is very helpful here.

After the child has spoken, if you feel it will be helpful, talk *briefly* and
respectfully about your viewpoint and feelings.

Transition Phrase:[9] Are you ready to think about things we might do to solve
this problem?

Brainstorm - Generate Ideas

Invite the child or children to work on finding solutions. Someone who
has been involved from the first step, identifying the problem, and who has
helped with solutions is far more likely to follow through with the agreed upon
solution than someone who has not.

It is important not to pass any judgments or make any criticism during brainstorming. Judgments stop the generation of ideas. All ideas need to be accepted for the time being. Often it is helpful to write down all of the ideas at this stage.

One of the early problems my family used problem solving on was to determine the children's bedtime and avoid the stalling and ugliness which had developed. The first idea my son Kris came up with was, "We'll just go to bed when we're tired." Clearly, to me this was not acceptable for a two and four year old. However, it was also obvious that we needed more ideas. If at this time I had said, "No, that won't work" or "I don't like this idea," my sons would have stopped thinking of more ideas. We wrote this first thought down and searched our minds for more ideas.

Transition Phrase:[9] Do you feel we have enough ideas to begin evaluating them?

Evaluate Options

Now it is time to evaluate the ideas - after many have been generated. Together, decide which ideas or portions of ideas you all feel comfortable with and which you do not like. Star or highlight the ideas you like best. Take time to make improvements on these promising ideas. Now is the time to modify, amend, or mix ideas. Be careful to avoid put-downs at this stage.

"I wouldn't be comfortable with that."
    or "I can live with this one."
Instead of:
    "This one is dumb."

Transition Phrase:[9] Do any of the solutions stand out as the best choice?

Select the Solution That Meets Everyone's Needs

When we select a solution that meets everyone's needs, we greatly increase the odds that everyone will follow through and comply with the decision. There is, however, a vast difference between a solution that meets everyone's needs and a compromise solution. Often, we stop at compromise rather than seeking further to find mutually agreeable. In *Getting to Yes*, Fisher and Ury suggest focusing on interests rather than positions to find a solution that meets everyone's needs. They tell a story about two men quarreling in a library:

> One wants the window open and the other wants it closed. They bicker back and forth about how much to leave it open: a crack, halfway, three quarters of the way. No solution satisfies them both.
> Enter the librarian. She asks one why he wants the window open: "To get some fresh air." She asks the other why he wants it closed: "To avoid the draft." After thinking a minute, she opens wide a window in the next room, bringing in fresh air without a draft.

We can learn much from this story. First, interests help to define the problem more clearly - to clarify the *real* problem (gain fresh air versus avoid draft), rather than the problem first stated (open window versus closed window), which involves positions. Second, if the parties involved had stayed with positions, the best solution they would have devised would have been a compromise position (window half open), where each gains some of what he wants and each loses some of what he wants. Neither is satisfied with the solution. Although it is no longer being addressed, in reality, there is still a problem. Third, in order to discover interests, the librarian asked, "Why?" ("Why do you want the window closed?" "Why do you want the window open?") Sometimes asking "Why not?" ("Why don't you want the window closed?" "Why don't you want the window open?") can be helpful as well. Lastly, the librarian used an important skill to invent the solution; she took a moment to *think*. She invented a solution for this specific problem.

> **Focus on interests, not positions, to define the core problem and uncover mutually agreeable solutions that last.**

Transition Phrase:[9] Are you ready to plan who does what by when?

Make a Specific Plan

Determine what steps need to be taken to get this plan into action. Decide who will be responsible for what - specifically. Set a time frame for completion of actions. Without the specifics of who, what, and when, excellent plans may fail. Be very clear.

Transition Phrase:[9] It might be helpful to think about how we'll know if your solution really works.

Provision for Review; Planning a Failsafe

How will you know if the solution really works and if you have been successful? Determine the critical factors to success. Agree to try the plan for a short, specific time (three days, a week, a morning), and then to evaluate progress. If the plan is not working, if all parties are not satisfied, return to the first step.

Transition Phrase:[9] I will check with you next Thursday.

No matter how calmly you try to referee, parenting will eventually produce bizarre behavior, and I'm not talking about the kids. *Their behavior is always normal.* - Bill Cosby, *Fatherhood*

9:
Temper Tantrums

Temper tantrums can be extremely difficult and time-consuming to handle. Traditionally, we have been taught to ignore them.   There are serious concerns about ignoring a child having a temper tantrum. The first concern centers on the reason children have temper tantrums. We must be very precise about what we label a temper tantrum because there are two very similar-looking behaviors that appear to be tantrums; only one qualifies as a true tantrum. In the pretend tantrum, a child is in perfect command of himself and is seeking attention or his own way. We generally get that feeling in the pit of our stomachs which says, "This does not ring true; it seems false. This feels like a performance." It is a performance. The key factor here is that the child is in command of himself and is directing his behavior.

When a child is in the midst of a true temper tantrum, he is no longer in command of his actions. Real temper tantrums are not to seek attention; they may, however, be an effort to get one's own way. True tantrums are the result of frustration and anger. Children enter these tantrums because the blocks fell down, they cannot get their shoestrings tied, they want a cookie but are not allowed to have one, they do not want to pick up toys. It is helpful to consider what happens physiologically to a child, or anyone, when anger takes over. Anger, like fear, triggers adrenalin. This triggering is an ancient survival mechanism. When a caveman, walking through the jungle, hears a sabre tooth tiger above him, his survival depends on the quickness of his response. Adrenalin enables reflexive action - no thought, no decision-making to slow down response time. The caveman either flings his spear or runs like crazy. Fight or flight. In order to deliver this reflexive action, adrenalin increases heart rate and respiration. Have you ever noticed how much stronger a child having a temper tantrum is? Perhaps more significantly, adrenalin shuts down the left hand portion of the brain to allow the right hand portion, where reflexive action is controlled, to dominate. The problem becomes clear when we realize that the left hand portion of the brain, which has been overridden, controls reason, logic, and language. This is why trying to reason with a child having a temper tantrum never works.

Perhaps the most important thing we can say to ourselves when dealing with anyone who is angry is, "No thinking person is home." Our first job is to help get the thinking person back. Neither discipline nor problem-solving can take place until the thinking person, in command of the left hand portion of their brain, returns. Ignoring does not help this important return. We must consider the message that ignoring a child in temper tantrum sends: "As long as you are in control of yourself, I will be there for you; but if you get out of control (and truly need my help), I will not be available to you. You are on your own in a time of great need."

Researchers have compared the brain wave patterns of many different groups of children; among those were children in temper tantrum. The brain wave patterns of children in temper tantrum most closely resembled the brain wave patterns of children in epileptic seizure. None of us would ever consider abandoning or ignoring a child during a seizure. Truly, there is no thinking person home.

In addition, many children begin to hurt themselves, others, or things (furniture, walls, toys) in the course of a tantrum. None of us allows this; we intervene immediately. Thus, we have not been ignoring. We end up teaching - teaching children to do the temper tantrum exactly the way we do not want it. We teach them to hurt something or someone in order to get our help and our recognition that there is a problem.

There are two important steps to handling temper tantrums. First, we must help the child calm down, reduce the anger, and get back the thinking portion of his brain. This is the difficult step because what works with one child may cause another child to go deeper into anger. Some children like to be held and rocked or to be hummed to; these types of activities which involve motion or music are right brain controlled. We must go through this right-hand, controlling side of the brain to help restart the left hand, reasonable side. Motion - swaying, rocking, and patting all help us calm down. Lullabies have been used for their calming effect since the beginning of time. Unfortunately, some children are made angrier by our touch or proximity. It is better to allow these children space as long as they hurt nothing. Allowing a child space is vastly different from ignoring a child and refusing to help. Still other children need to use up the energy the adrenalin has given them. These children run, stomp, pound, and jump.

It would be wonderful if there were an easy way to determine what works best with any given child. However, trial and error is the only method to find out what works. The first step in dealing with a child in temper tantrum is to find a way to help him calm down.

Step two is to return to the initiating event and take appropriate disciplinary action or problem-solving steps. We want to teach the child that the temper tantrum will neither prevent him from doing what he did not want nor get him what he did want. In other words, if the temper tantrum was about not wanting to pick up toys, this child will return to pick up the same toys. If the tantrum was initiated by blocks falling down, then yelling, crying, and hitting someone else will not get the blocks back into position. Temper tantrums do not get you what you want, nor do they solve problems. This is an important lesson children, and some adults, must learn.

Learning to handle our anger appropriately is a job all of us continue to try to complete. We must help children begin to recognize developing anger and begin to learn how to handle it. Skills develop over time. A three year old may appropriately stamp her foot; a nine year old needs to use appropriate verbal skills or to isolate herself for a time until she can cope better. We cannot rid our lives of frustration and anger; we can learn to handle them appropriately, respectfully, and responsibly.

Time-out

This leads us directly to time-out. Despite what you have been taught, time-out, by itself, is *NOT* a discipline tool. It is, however, a truly indispensable tool used *prior to* discipline or problem solving. First, let us investigate the confusion surrounding time-out, then we will address the remarkable tool itself.

When time-out is incorrectly taught as a child management tool, it is suggested that we place a child in time-out, generally a chair, for any and all digressions. What lesson does sitting a child down in a separate place for *any misbehavior* teach a child? It can teach that a child can do something negative to someone whose actions they do not like. It can teach resentment, and it can teach attention-seeking. But it will not teach any correct principles or helpful life lessons which are required for DISCIPLINE.

Time-out improperly used as child management falls into the category of *punishment.* It has been confused with *isolation,* which is a discipline tool used specifically as a consequence for a child having difficulty getting along with other children. Isolation (not time-out) is suggested for use when a child who is not upset is having difficulty getting along with friends playing together. Picture this, Amy tries to color on Martha's Mother's Day picture. Martha realizes what is about to happen, and in trying to prevent Amy from ruining her picture, Martha pushes Amy off her chair. Martha is not upset; she solved her problem. Amy has not ruined her picture. Both children require discipline. Both may be separated from their friends at the table because each is having difficulty working nicely together. The consequence involved is: You have a choice: You can choose to play appropriately at the table and continue staying with your friends, or you can choose to try to mark on your friend's papers (play inappropriately) and play at another table by yourself (away from temptation) in *isolation.* This is a specific technique for a specific type of misbehavior. It teaches an important life lesson about getting along with other children or needing to play by yourself. It also teaches about avoiding temptation where possible.

What then is time-out? As the word itself suggests, originally time-out was a gift of time and space given to *upset* children. The key is that the child is in emotional distress. It is time away from regular activities. Misbehaving children do not go to time-out: upset children do. They enter time-out, which can be a chair or set place, but need not be, to calm themselves down, to find the thinking person. I have seen time-out chairs called sugar chairs, where one goes to find one's sweet self. I have seen benches with banners behind them declaring, "Please don't talk to me; I am trying to get myself back together." These all represent time-out.

Time-out, to be most helpful, must be followed by discipline or problem solving. Once the child is calm and able to think, discipline (when you pick up the clay, then you may get out the building blocks) or problem solving can take place. The issue which caused the distress or tempter tantrum must be addressed, not ignored.

> ☞ Time-out is an excellent tool for helping children calm down, often the first step for dealing with tantrums. Redirection is a common form of discipline which follows time-out with younger children. Problem solving is most common with older children.

During a seminar, a pre-school teacher asked me about having used time-out slightly differently. Near the end of one of those extremely long days, she found herself quite upset with one particular student. As she started to walk toward this student, she realized that what she was about to say was unhelpful and hurtful. Rather than continue toward him, she walked herself to the time-out chair and sat down in it. She asked me if she had done the right thing. I asked her to describe what had happened when she sat down. As expected, her entire classroom settled down, became very quiet, and stared open-mouthed at their teacher in the time-out chair. So far so good. After a short time in this chair, the teacher felt calmer and returned to teaching. I asked her if in the next few days anything unusual had occurred in her classroom. It seems that the next day, one of her students found himself very mad at another student. The teacher watched as the irate student eyed the other, clenched his fists, and then slowly but deliberately walked to the time-out chair and sat down - just as his teacher had done the day before. A short time later, after calming down, he went back to work. The teacher asked me if this was alright. I answered that it was wonderful. She had modeled what we all need to do when we are angry - take time to calm down before we proceed. In other words, use time-out. It is fine when we offer to provide time-out for angry children; it is even better, a sign of maturity, if they provide it for themselves. Great modeling tends to produce great lessons.

Time-out teaches an extremely important principle: When we are angry and bent out of shape, we have the right to do nothing. First calm down, then make decisions and take actions. We tend to regret almost everything we ever say and do when we are angry. It is better to be silent and inactive and need neither to regret our actions nor to apologize for them. Situations involving domestic disputes are a leading cause of police officers' deaths. These extreme examples involve someone who is very angry and has failed to learn the correct principle of time-out.

Time-out is a gift of time and space which teaches: Take no action while angry. First take time to calm down.

Each of us needs to learn how to use time-out and then how, on our own, to place ourselves in time-out. Remember, time-out is not for misbehavior; time-out is for distress. It is a gift.

It may prove helpful to work through the exercises on the following pages.

Discipline Practice - Parents
Pre-School & School Age

For each situation described, respond to the following questions: 1)How I feel right now about this child. 2)What I generally first say. 3)What I might say that would be more helpful. 4)What I usually say next. 5)What I might say that would be more helpful. 6)What I do next. 7)What might be more effective. 8)Trap I fall into or mistake I usually make. 9)How can I avoid this?

1. Mark and Rob are fighting over who will hold the television remote control.

2. You look up and see Sheila smack Terry.

3. Robbie does not want to go to bed; he wants to play longer.

4. Jane says she will not eat her cauliflower. She means it!

5. Joshua has forgotten to make his bed again or left out his toys again.

6. You leave your two daughters for fifteen minutes while you talk to a neighbor; they have eaten candy, destroyed the family room, and one of them is hurt.

7. Melissa is bothering her brother again.

8. Sally tells you that the two other neighborhood girls won't let her play.

Discipline Practice - Parents
Teens

For each situation described, respond to the following questions: 1)How I feel right now about this child. 2)What I generally first say. 3)What I might say that would be more helpful. 4)What I usually say next. 5)What I might say that would be more helpful. 6)What I do next. 7)What might be more effective. 8)Trap I fall into or mistake I usually make. 9)How can I avoid this?

1. Mark and Rob are fighting over who will get the car.

2. You look up and see your teen push your youngest child.

3. Despite your reminders and requests, Rob still has not taken out the trash.

4. It is 10:00p.m.; your daughter tells you she forgot about her science homework.

5. Joshua needs new jeans; he wants the most expensive designer jeans.

6. You leave your oldest son in charge of starting dinner while you run to the store. When you return, you find him on the phone with no dinner started.

7. Melissa continues to put-down her younger brother.

8. Sally tells you that her older brother is making fun of her new swimsuit.

Discipline Practice -
Early Childhood Educators

For each situation described, respond to the following questions: 1)How I feel right now about this child. 2)What I generally first say. 3)What I might say that would be more helpful. 4)What I usually say next. 5)What I might say that would be more helpful. 6)What I do next. 7)What might be more effective. 8)Trap I fall into or mistake I usually make. 9)How can I avoid this?

1. Mark and Rob are fighting over who will use the blue crayon first.

2. You look up and see Sheila smack Terry.

3. Robbie does not want to go to his next activity; he wants to continue building block towers.

4. Jane says she will not go to a different center. She means it!

5. Joshua has left toys all over, again.

6. Clay just scribbled all over Sarah's picture.

7. Melissa is bothering Sheila, again.

8. Sally tells you that John just took her ball.

Discipline Practice -
Teachers

For each situation described, respond to the following questions: 1)How I feel right now about this student. 2)What I generally first say. 3)What I might say that would be more helpful. 4)What I usually say next. 5)What I might say that would be more helpful. 6)What I do next. 7)What might be more effective. 8)Trap I fall into or mistake I usually make. 9)How can I avoid this?

1. A student is not participating, has no book or pencil, and refuses to work on the assignment or open his book.

2. A student is beginning to clown around or verbally disrupt your class.

3. Right before class starts, Sally tells you that John just took her book.

4. During class, a student says, "I don't have to listen to you!"

5. A student contradicts you on a point of information.

6. You notice a student moseying along; you tell him to hurry or he will be late for class. He says, "yeah, right, whatever," and continues his slow pace.

7. Mark and Rob are fighting over who will use the pencil sharpener first.

8. You look up and see Sheila smack Terry.

10:
Discipline Summary

To do things today exactly the way you did them yesterday saves thinking. - Woodrow Wilson

Of course, nothing will change or improve either. Thinking is necessary to discipline children. There is no easy way out.

There you have it, over one hundred different phrasings and actions to handle various situations and children. Still, we have not covered it all. I know you were hoping I would be "THE ONE" - the one who would solve all of your discipline concerns, the one who would fix the children, the one who would make life with children easy. I wish I could place my hand on your forehead and "heal," but I cannot. "THE ONE" does not exist. The magic cookbook approach has not been written and cannot be. We all hope for that one guaranteed formula - if you will just do this, this, and this, your children will be perfect or at least turn out fine and your life will be easy.

Being a parent, rearing children, being a teacher, running a classroom, disciplining - all require *thinking*. There simply is no way around this fact. We must make judgment calls (what to ignore, who is telling the truth, how important is this issue?) almost constantly. Further, we must determine what each child needs to learn, decide exactly what principles are important to us and our future, and find and use words or actions which effectively teach these principles and improve behavior. This is not easy. It is, in fact, extraordinarily difficult. In addition, the job continues to change. The children are constantly changing. Parenting a toddler is not the same as parenting a teen. Being a parent or a teacher is a process oriented job. No one is ever completely formed. We change constantly throughout our life. This is the reason all of us, even the brightest, most principled, most caring of us, struggle with discipline. There is, however, good news.

Using DISCIPLINE FOR *LIFE!*, investment discipline, discipline based in respect, discipline based on correct principles can and will make life with children easier, more fulfilling, more joyful and enjoyable, more relaxed and comfortable now and in the long run. Your integrity *can* be intact. You *can* be competent and confident. You *can* be who you want to be!

Our goal or vision for our discipline program must be clear. If it is not, we are headed into a *future we allowed to happen rather than one we shaped.* It is critical that each of us takes time and determines what principles we believe in and wish to teach to our children. We must be aware that life lessons are always being taught - *whether or not we are aware of them.* It is far more prudent and beneficial to be aware.

We can no longer afford to 'fight fires'. It is our job to stop and check what we actually are teaching and to teach only what we believe. Our own responsibility and ownership are clear.

There is yet one last level of discipline. The first level regards discipline as what we do to change children's behavior. It merely addresses changing behavior right now. Built upon this layer is the second level of discipline which views discipline as more far-reaching in that it teaches: lessons, life lessons, correct principles to guide lives, healthy relationships, and respectful communication. The third level, which is built on the first two layers, considers that discipline, specifically how each of us chooses to discipline, tells who we are. My disciplinary actions identify and disclose who I am quite clearly and certainly. Regardless of whether I am tired, frustrated, or stressed, whether I have taken time to learn and develop skills, whether I like it or not, and whether I am aware of it or not, I own how I discipline. Whenever we discipline, we teach and we reveal who we really are. This brings us right back to our own integrity (which is where I started.) We must ask ourselves, "Do I act on and practice what I believe in, or are my beliefs and actions on two different courses?" Do I, or do I not, have integrity?

Discipline truly is about *teaching*. A child in need of discipline always creates an OPPORTUNITY FOR LEARNING and thus for TEACHING. True discipline must ask, *What lesson needs to be learned here; how can I best teach it to this child?"* True discipline is based on correct principles.

Of course, we need to be wise about what we select to teach. Among the most important are those included in the Corsini Four-R System (C4R):

FOUR R'S
RESPECT - the key to cooperation, dignity, and worth.

RESPONSIBILITY - the foundation under all of discipline is ownership of behavior, the belief that *I am responsible for what I choose to do and for what happens to me and others as a result.* We not only have the right to choose our behavior, we have an obligation.

RESOURCEFULNESS - the liberator who empowers us to take charge of our lives in new ways. No more helplessness!

RESPONSIVENESS - the deterrent that keeps us human and humane. Some of our darkest periods in history were led by those who had an abundance of the first three traits, but none of this one.

Please keep in mind the Law of the Harvest:

If we compel children to submit by trying to control them, we will reap a future where violence and abuse of power continue to grow. They will simple ask, "Who can stop me?"

If we continue to reward children, we must accept a future filled with people who care only about themselves, who make decisions based on immediate self-interest, and who are willing to manipulate others to accomplish their own purposes. They will ask, "What's in it for me?"

If we constantly punish children and make them pay, they will become resentful, bitter people who frequently find it necessary to work against others. Further, they are controlled only by outside forces, who must be watching and able to do something *to* them. All that will matter is, "Will I get caught?"

But if we *TEACH* our children how to conduct their lives responsibly, respectfully, healthfully, and if we *TEACH* our children healthy life messages (I like myself, I can think for myself, There is no problem so great I cannot handle it), we will reap also what we have sown. Here and only here does our future look much brighter.

Sounds great, makes sense, but will it work? Yes, it will - **one step at a time**....

The Law of the Farm is true for us and for children as well. J.G. Hubbard summed it up this way: "One thing at a time, all things in succession. That which grows slowly endures." Parenting, teaching, learning to deal with children helpfully is a process. We must acquire patience and meet this challenge one step at a time. Growth takes time.

Our legacy: The next generation will be closer to where we need to be, not farther into chaos. It has been noted that Buckminster Fuller described our job as that of the trim tab on a sail boat. With slight adjustments to the trim tab, the rudder moves. With adjustments to the rudder, the ship moves. Our legacy will be a nation closer to harbor, not farther out in the stormy sea. One child at a time, one day at a time, we move closer to safe harbor. Our generation may not get the ship to harbor; we can, however, teach the next generation well enough that they will get home safely. Not a bad legacy.

> The future will depend on what we do in the present.
> - Ghandi

THE LESSON OF THE PIE

We have looked at discipline closely; we have considered the absolute seriousness of this vast, crucial undertaking. And we have looked at many ways to help teach our children the important life lessons they will need. But let us never overlook the lesson of humanity and laughter and fun. Some of us get lost in the job of parenting or teaching; we take it and ourselves much too seriously and lose ourselves and sometimes our children in the process. My absolute favorite and most cherished discipline strategy comes from, of all places, a television commercial viewed years ago. Here is my memory of this commercial.

On a bright, summer day a mother and daughter have just returned from grocery shopping in the family station wagon. The daughter is helping her mom carry in the grocery bags when she drops one, the one with the fresh apple pie. Her mother turns and sees the calamity, but before she speaks, this scenario is interrupted to talk to us about the importance of children and parenting.

If we stop here, many of you, having taken the message about life lessons seriously (as I meant for you to), will anticipate what needs to be done. The daughter just needs to understand that she is responsible for her action; she has simply made a mistake for which she needs to make amends. She could replace dessert by baking or fixing something else for the family. Mom may or may not help depending on her other duties and the lesson she wants to teach (self-sufficiency or help in times of need). Sounds good. But the producers of the commercial were far wiser. *Sometimes wisdom and humanity are very hard to find.*

When the commercial returns to the car scene, the mother and daughter are sitting on the tail gate happily eating the smashed pie. They remembered another important life lesson: "When life gives you lemons, make lemonade," or more apropos, when you smash a pie, eat it quick. Mom understands that her child is considerably more important than the pie, and that special moments need to be recognized and treasured.

By no means does this book cover all the lessons your children will need. Please do not overlook the most important ones - the humane lessons, the lessons which understand that our children are *gifts*. For our children are people, too. We are allowed to have fun with them and enjoy them. In fact, it is essential that we do so. Perhaps to the enjoinder, "stop and smell the roses," we should add, "stop and smell the children." Well, perhaps, "stop and enjoy the children." Like the roses, children do not last long. They grow up. They find lives for themselves. And we will miss them. They are a special gift and presence. The elderly, read experienced, venerable, and wiser than the young, understand this. They take time with children; sometimes, they simply sit and watch them. They understand just how precious a child is. Life offers no more precious gift.

PART IV - BUILDING SELF-ESTEEM

11:
The Importance of Self Esteem

> This above all: to thine own self be true, and it must follow
> as the night the day, thou canst not then be false to any
> man. - William Shakespeare

Why Self-Esteem is Critical

The final discipline technique to be addressed is ENHANCE SELF-ESTEEM. The
strong links between discipline and self-esteem are clear. The better, more
respectful and humane, the discipline, the higher the self-esteem. The higher
a child's self-esteem, the more infrequent her misbehavior and the easier the
discipline. This is a major reason to try to build self-esteem. More important,
however, is the fact that the higher self-esteem, the healthier the child and
later in life, the adult.

Do you ever wonder if something is missing? Do you ever find yourself
believing you are worthless or incapable?   Do contentment, joy, and
confidence elude you? Do you wish you could be someone else? You are
not alone. And sadly, more and more children feel this way. When I talk with
teachers across the nation, they concur that self-esteem is declining -
conspicuously, both in adults and children. This is an alarming trend. As
self-esteem declines, so too does our nation. Our nation needs positiveness,
confidence, and courage; these traits are correlated with high self-esteem.

Keys to Life

In *The Psychology of Self Esteem*, Nathaniel Branden says,

> There is no value judgment more important to man, no factor more decisive in his psychological development and motivation - than the estimate he passes on himself. The nature of his self evaluation has profound effects on a man's thinking processes, emotion, desires, values and goals. It is the single most significant key to his behavior.

This is a powerful statement. It mirrors Dorothy Briggs' assertion in *Your Child's Self-Esteem* that:

> Self-esteem is the mainspring that slates every child for success or failure as a human being.

If you agree with these statements, then a crucial job for every parent and every teacher is affirming and building self-esteem in each child. None of us had children or chose to work with them in order to make them feel worse. In fact, a cardinal trait found in most caregivers and educators is that they chose their profession because *they want to make a positive difference in children's lives*. I have seen a poster in a school which read - All children have the right to discover that within them they have the power to learn how to learn and how to think and how to handle their lives with courage and confidence. As teachers, we owe our students at least this much. As parents, our responsibility is even greater for we are the single most significant influence in our children's lives. As Dorothy Briggs asserts, "Helping children build high self-esteem is the key to successful parenthood."

It is also the key to successful teaching. As the book by Aspy and Roebuck entitled *Kids Don't Learn From People They Don't Like* suggests, how we view, value, and treat children affects how much they learn from us. Each of us remembers a year in high school when we had one teacher we adored and one we did not like at all. We learned more, our grades were higher, and we enjoyed and behaved in class more with the teacher we liked - no matter what the subject. Alternatively, we learned less with what seemed like more effort, had difficulty paying attention and behaving, and loathed class with the teacher we felt did not like us and whom we, in turn, learned to dislike.

Most importantly, high self-esteem is a key to emotional health. Liking ourselves and feeling capable are the foundations on which emotional health rests. High self-esteem is simply the key to our lives. How can a child recognize her own goodness and her gifts if her parents do not? If her teachers do not? This is clearly a monumental responsibility, not to be taken lightly. Our job then is to help children feel better about themselves, not worse. How can we do this?

Research, among it the work of Stanley Coopersmith, shows that self-esteem develops from the quality of the relationships between a child and those (parent, care-giver, teacher, grandparent) who play a significant role in his life. Children, at one time, were considered to be blank slates upon which we write. The environment, it was believed, shaped the child entirely. Yet, any parent of more than one child and every teacher realize children differ from each other from the start. We will not revisit the nature-nurture debate here. Nature certainly contributes; we each come into the world different, unique. Nature provides the groundwork, the clay (some malleable, some less so, some light and full of sun, others gloomier and full of clouds); nurture provides the molding and shaping. It is indisputable that environmental factors, other people, circumstances, and events, modify the original model. Nurture does affect what nature gave us. Another perceptive analogy describes us, parents, caregivers, and teachers, as the mirror our children look into to learn who they are and what value they have.

What do we want then? A child who is deeply and quietly happy to be himself.

Every child, despite her uniqueness, has two basic psychological needs: to feel loveable and to feel capable. Many experts agree that these two basic human needs translate into two convictions:

I am lovable: I have value because I exist

I am capable: I can handle myself and my environment

Notice that what is important is not that the child is loved but that he feels loved. Parents cannot simply love a child in their hearts; they must be able to demonstrate this love so that a child truly feels loved. Each child from infancy needs to be told with words and actions that she is loveable and important. Parents must accept this responsibility.

Sadly, not all do. That is when teachers become even more important in a child's life. Teachers are the second most important influence on a child's life. Many caregivers and teachers spend more time and have more interaction and communication with a child than his parents. For some children, a teacher is the only positive person they regularly encounter. We must be aware of what messages we are actually sending, and we must become very skilled at sending the correct messages. Do we view and thus portray diaper changing time as a nuisance job to be finished in record time? As a time to send the message, "I wish you weren't here; your existence is not important." Or is it a loving time, a time to tickle, stroke, and talk to your baby? A time to send once more the critical message that your baby is loved, important, irreplaceable? No one expects you to enjoy the diaper part, but it is critical that you enjoy the baby part. *Take care that your baby does not receive the diaper's message!*

When your toddler tries a new skill, perhaps climbing a chair to be closer to you and the counter where you are working, do you send a you-are-not-capable message: "Get down off that chair! You'll fall and get hurt!" Or do you send a more affirming message, "You did it! And you were careful."

There is no doubt we are the mirrors from which our children learn who they are and how much value they have. It is the child's feelings about being loveable and capable that develop from our messages that help a child build self-esteem.

Three Categories of Self-Esteem

We discussed earlier that there are three LIFE BELIEFS (convictions or attitudes which children need to develop about themselves); these were: I like myself, I can think and do for myself, There is no problem so great I cannot handle it.

These three important LIFE BELIEFS parallel the three categories of self-esteem; these areas are Existence, Accomplishment, and Mistakes.[10]

I like myself	⇨	**Existence**
I can think and do for myself	⇨	**Accomplishment**
There is no problem so great I cannot handle it	⇨	**Mistakes**

The connection between these three areas of self-esteem and the two convictions based on human needs is also clear. I Am Lovable coincides with the area of Existence. The conviction I Am Capable involves both successes - Accomplishments and the other side of the coin, failures - Mistakes.

Two of the categories are concerned with what we do, with actions. The area of Accomplishment focuses on success - challenges we master. The third category, Mistakes, deals with our actions that have failed or gone awry. Each of us has experiences in both categories. It is a common misconception that the more accomplishments achieved and the fewer mistakes made, the greater one's self-esteem. Not so, self-esteem can be built and affirmed in all categories, including times when mistakes take place.

Quite significantly, though often overlooked, one section of self-esteem is not dependent upon actions. Self-esteem in Existence has to do with the fact that we each have value simply because we exist. We do not have to *do* anything to obtain this. We care about and care for a baby, *any baby*, deposited on a doorstep, not because of what the baby does (hardly!) but because it is there, it exists. This child has value simply because she has entered our lives, because she *is*.

Existence is the most fundamental and foundational area of self-esteem, upon which the other two areas are built.

The other two areas, Accomplishments and Mistakes, are built upon this first area. Without this primary one, self-esteem built solely on the other two is always unsteady, at risk, and mercurial. Self-esteem built without the stabilizing effects of affirmed existence is extremely vulnerable. Arthur Miller describes our proclivity to determine value based on success:

> Success instead of giving freedom of choice, becomes a way of life. There's no country I've been to where people, when you come into a room and sit down with them, so often ask, "What do you do?" And being American, many's the time I've almost asked that question, then realized it's good for my soul not to know. For a while! Just to let the evening wear on and see what I think of this person without knowing what he does and how successful he is, or what a failure. We're *ranking* everybody every minute of the day.

In our culture, as in many cultures, we overuse and overrate Accomplishments. (Just watch television, read the newspaper, listen to the first questions of people just meeting.) We place entirely too much significance on our successes. Consequently, we misuse the third category Mistakes; we lower our value when we make a mistake. As well, we sabotage and then proceed to underuse and underrate the value we have based purely on our Existence. As soon as a baby is born, we check to see if the baby can focus and track with his eyes; we get excited when the baby lifts her head or smiles (even if it is just gas). We are always waiting for the next accomplishment, and we quickly march right through the value of existing without ever noticing it or acknowledging it. Many of us do this on a daily basis. This is most unfortunate and detrimental.

Each of us knows a child or an adult whose self-esteem is built almost entirely on Accomplishments. These people are stressed constantly, and their value is at risk continuously. Why? We all know about mistakes. Everyone makes them. Everyone. When is the next mistake coming? No one knows, but we all know with a certainty that it is waiting just around the corner for us. When a child whose value rests on Accomplishments does well, self-esteem seems high; in truth, it is artificially high. But when that child is not successful (misses the catch, comes in second, gets a low grade), self-esteem plummets. And we then spend much time and energy trying to raise self-esteem back to its previous level. Again, we focus mostly on accomplishments further causing and aggravating the next fall. If, on the other hand, a child has 80% of his value based on Existence and he happens to make a mistake, his self-esteem can drop only a little - down to the 80% base level. And fairly quickly, on its own, self-esteem returns.

Let us look at the game of baseball, a game of heroes and goats. Much of the time during the game, the play is elsewhere. You are either up to bat or you are not. The ball is in your area or not. But when the play is in your area, you are on display. Have you ever been a center fielder? You frequently have fly balls arrive in your field. If you catch it, you are a hero - at least temporarily. If you drop it, you are a goat.

Imagine two center fielders: one whose self-esteem is built largely on accomplishments and one who has 90% of his self-esteem built on existence. The first fielder catches the ball, makes the out, and returns to the dugout like a returning king; of course, some of his teammates may not feel like bowing down in homage. This may cause some squabbling and dissension on the bench. The next inning this same fielder may not be so lucky. The ball flies toward him; he puts out his glove, and the ball hits and then bounces out of it. He returns to the dugout at the end of the inning like a wounded bear. Depending on his age and personality, he sulks, cries, swears, stomps the dirt, or yells at somebody else. He is less than pleasant to himself, his coach, and his teammates. Often his game goes downhill from here. And hope this was not an away game, because this child is not a joy to have in the car on the drive home. It is quite understandable; this child's estimation of his own worth has been yanked around by outside events from very high to almost nothing. He is bound to be stressed and disagreeable. In truth, this child really does not know what he is worth; his value is always changing, always at risk. Is it any wonder he grasps at any accomplishment to feel good? Or is willing to lie or cheat or make excuses to feel good? ("The sun was in my eyes. I couldn't see the ball.")

Briggs, in *Your Child's Self-Esteem*, notes that "whenever personal worth is dependent upon performance, personal value is subject to cancellation with every misstep."

Bryan Forbes formed an interesting truth in the twist of a phrase:
"Nothing recedes like success."

Let us return to baseball and our second center fielder. This is the one who understands he is valuable simply because he exists; this allows him to also understand baseball is a *game*. When he makes a catch, he returns to the dugout happy and accepts the hoorays and pats from his coach and team; after all, it is fun to catch the ball - to accomplish and succeed. It is also short-lived, and that is alright, too. This player does not get lost in it. He might even tell the second baseman about her great play. Inevitably, another inning, another fly ball, this time, a missed catch. This child's estimate of his value drops - a little. That is all it can drop. And without question, he wishes he had caught the ball. He walks back to the dugout wondering if maybe what the coach said about using two hands merits trying. He may sit down quietly for a while, but pretty soon he recovers. He walks over to his friend the catcher, with whom he is spending the night, and asks, "Do we really get to order pizza tonight? What's your favorite place? Do you like Canadian bacon on it?" He is back, and he is whole and valuable. And we will not mind having him with us; he is all ready for a good time.

OVER-EMPHASIS ON ACCOMPLISHMENT

Stress on accomplishment has taken a toll on many: both sexes are involved, but we continue to be especially hard on men. Too many of us have most of our self-esteem tied up in the most visible form of accomplishment or success - our jobs. We have convincingly taught ourselves that the dollars we bring home are inextricably linked to our worth. If our job is not good enough (high power or high status) or high paying enough, our worth is less. And, if we should happen to lose our job, we are in danger of losing most of our value as a person. Evidently, we are genuinely in danger.

Perhaps you are fortunate to not know anyone who has taken his own life. Many of us are not so lucky. I am not. The last two funerals I attended were for men who had committed suicide. One of the two men whose death haunts my thoughts had a dispute with his boss and lost or left his job. That afternoon, he took his own life. I do not pretend to know what goes through anyone's mind at a time like this, certainly, many factors. But the timing of this suicide makes it difficult to dispute that not having a job was one of the contributing factors, perhaps a prompting factor. For too many men, no job equals no value. No value equals no need for existence. No need for existence equals no life. We must stop this type of thinking. However, it seems that rather than reducing it, we are now effectively spreading it to women. After this incident, which stunned and frightened every woman in one of my parent groups (no one is immune), each woman decided to make sure that her husband understood or began to understand that his value does not come from the paycheck he brings home, but from the fact that he brings himself home each evening. As we all know, previous bias or learning can be difficult to override.   Nevertheless, we must stop over-emphasizing accomplishments.

This was still too expensive a lesson.

OVER-EMPHASIS ON APPEARANCE

Much as we try not to, it is evident that we continue to treat boys and girls differently. They *are* different. Testosterone and estrogen are two very different hormones. Male and female 'nature' are different; male and female 'nurture' need not be.   Many arenas of life are affected by these dissimilarities. For example, research shows us that, generally, boys seek a teacher's notice more aggressively than do girls. As a result, teachers, quite inadvertently, tend to call on boys more often. This is certainly not the only occurrence where the adage "the squeaky wheel gets the grease" is given life.

What we seek is beneficial treatment for each child. The issue at hand is providing the necessary affirmations of self-esteem for every child. All children need to receive many different affirmations encompassing all three areas of self-esteem. Which affirmations we choose to offer a child may inadvertently be determined by his or her gender rather than by his or her individual needs. Previously we discussed how boys are more at risk for linking most of their self-esteem to success and accomplishments. They receive more affirmations in this area of self-esteem, and as a result, assume accomplishment is most important in establishing self-worth.

By contrast, girls generally receive more affirmations in the area of existence, primarily receiving messages that highlight the importance of appearance. We are far more likely to tell a little girl we think she is pretty, that her hair looks nice, or that her outfit is lovely than a boy. For some of us, it may even be difficult to imagine saying these things to a boy. Furthermore, we are less likely to validate a girl about her ability to cope, her accomplishments, or her successes. We seem more comfortable allowing a girl to be helpless than we do a boy. Some girls fail to receive enough messages that they can *do* things, and that they can be and should expect to be capable, effective and productive. Sadly, as a result, some females tie most of their value into their looks which, as we all recognize, are destined to fade. Little of their value comes from their abilities or their existence. Some take desperate actions trying to look beautiful, yet fail to develop skills that last a lifetime. We must ensure that we give all children positive messages about their abilities to cope, to think for themselves, to handle problems, to conduct and own their lives. It is important to remember that we most frequently fail to do so with our girls. It is critical that girls and boys receive affirmations in all three areas and based on their individual needs, not on our own unrecognized gender bias.

The second and third categories of self-esteem, Accomplishments and Mistakes, are inextricably tied together. We all know we feel better about ourselves when we do something right. Accomplishing feels good and builds our self-esteem. However, the other side is that doing something wrong, making mistakes, frequently makes us feel less valuable, less good about ourselves. *This is not necessary.* Interestingly, the area of Mistakes provides the opportunity for the most dramatic and quickest increase in self-esteem. Consider how it feels when we accomplish something or get something right easily and quickly. Most of us feel good and enjoy the success. However, each of us has messed something up, missed what we needed to do, and had to grapple and struggle with a challenge. Perhaps we had to learn, acquire skills, seek help. But in the end, we finally conquer our mistake and make things right. (Let's just say we got parenting or teaching right.) How does it feel when we straighten things out? When we get things right which previously we had gotten wrong? Wonderful! It is more fun to beat a tough adversary than a weak one.

When we compare the three categories of self-esteem, we realize that:

Existence is the foundation of self-esteem. Without self-esteem in this area, a child is at risk and will have difficulty building lasting self-esteem in the other categories.

Accomplishment is the most fleeting area, and when over-affirmed has a tendency to overshadow and place at risk the other two areas of self-esteem.

Mistakes provides the quickest boost to self-esteem, yet it is the most abused area, for we often reduce self-esteem within this category.

It is necessary to learn how to affirm children in all three of these categories of self-esteem. It must also be clear that the one area of self-esteem that everyone needs first and foremost is Existence - the one we so frequently and habitually overlook and skip by without ever noticing. Let us begin with this all-important realm of self-esteem.

12:
Existence

LIFE MESSAGE: I Am Valuable - I Am Lovable - I am Likeable
TRAIT: Positiveness

> The healthy child is true to himself; this gives him personal integrity. He does what he can with what he has and is at peace within. The unhealthy one lives by borrowed standards. At odds with himself, he masks his unacceptable parts and judges himself and others accordingly. - D.C. Briggs

Self-worth must not come just from achievements; it comes from our acceptance of each child just as she is. Each child must have fundamental worth *separate* from accomplishments and mistakes. We must help our children realize that they have value simply because they exist.

At bedtime one night, I, rather foolhardily, asked my younger son a seemingly innocent and easy question - one to which I was certain he knew the answer. "If I could choose from all of the children in the world, whom would I choose to have for my child?" Now because I had already told him a million times that I loved him, I assumed he would blurt out the only answer conceivable - him. Not so.

He looked at me and disclosed, "Probably one like me but better behaved." (Well, yes, there is some emphasis on good behavior at our house.) I was astounded and saddened; the answer was so very clear to me. How could *he* not know? Easily, I had never told him. I did not recover as quickly as I would have liked.

I responded, "No, really, who would I choose?"

"A good one, one who behaves all the time," he said.

I finally recouped, and I told him my heartfelt truth. "No, darling, I would choose you without ever needing to look at any of the others; *I would choose you.*"

"I don't always do the right thing; I don't always behave," he reconfided.

"I know," I said. "That doesn't matter at all, and it isn't the point. The point is that you are my first choice for a child; I want you; I would choose *you.*"

He thought about it for a moment and then asked me why. I should have seen this one coming. Don't ask the first question unless you know why. Luckily, I did.

"Because you are my son, because you are *you*, because although you don't belong to me, you belong with me. We are family. No one can ever take your place." He thought again for a moment, digesting what I had said, I thought.

And then he, of course, asked, "If you could only choose one, would you choose me or my brother?" I should have seen this one coming, too. By now, I was thinking as fast as I could. I found this truth more quickly.

"I'd choose two - both of you. I would not go away with only one. I came with two; I take two away. Period." He accepted this answer.

The point is that to believe in himself, a child must not have to question his worth as a person. - D.C. Briggs

Telling our children we love them is exceedingly important, but it is not enough. We need repeatedly to reaffirm their value based purely on existence. How can we do this?

Greetings

Greet them at each reunion and acknowledge them throughout the day.

Greeting - it seems so simple. We underestimate its power, and we, at times, fail to do it appropriately. First, greetings have power. One of my early career positions was not fun. The working environment was polarized and negative. I remember feeling down and less than valuable. I had naively expected that my boss would always appreciate me. I sought reassurance and solace at my friend Linda's house at lunch times. Linda was always glad to see me; bless her heart. But it was her baby daughter Sarah who always managed to greet me first. Sarah was still in a walker and raced to the door when she heard the knock and my entrance. With a big smile, she greeted me with, "Hi Malm!" - the best she could do with my difficult name. I always felt better immediately. For Sarah, like her mother, was just glad to see *me*; what a gift.

My husband, too, has taught me about greeting. My work with parents takes me out evenings. Tired, I arrive home. My husband has been known to hear the garage door open and come to the back door, open my car door, take my briefcase, and tell me he is glad I am home. He often offers to make me a cup of tea or cocoa. The long day washes away - at least partly, and I realize how very glad I am to be home and that someone cares about me.

Do you know who are the best greeters in the world? Dogs. They are the only ones who will get up from a nap, walk over to us, and with all their body language (tail wagging) tell us they are glad to see us. Inevitably, we put down our things and reach down to pat them. And somewhere in our minds and our hearts, we think, "At least *someone's* glad I'm home."

A preschool teacher at one of my presentations told me that when the young children arrive in her classroom, they always come over to her and show her their shoes or shirts or hair bows. She wondered how she should respond. Should she tell them how beautiful their hair is or how nice their shirt looks? We probed the incidents and determined that the children were not seeking praise. What they wanted and needed was *reconnection* to her as they were leaving Mom or Dad and *acknowledgment* that each was important to her. They were checking the emotional climate. Is it safe? Is it nurturing? Is it affirming? It is not just attention they wanted, but affection and affirmation.   What they want and need to know is that they are important and loveable, that they belong here, and that they are emotionally safe - not that their shirt is cute.   She decided that a hug or a smile and an "I'm glad you're here today," were what was most helpful.

Our greetings to others tell much about us and our feelings toward the person being greeted. If you are a teacher busily looking for a file you need for today's program and one of your favorite parents, Mrs. Sunny, walks by your room, I will wager you will stick your finger in the file cabinet to hold your place and turn and call out your greeting. This parent brings sunshine into your life, she will respond with a smile and friendly retort which makes you smile, and you always have time to collect a little sun.   But when Mrs. Grumpy walks past, most likely you just stick your head farther into the file cabinet; after all, you are busy preparing for class. We do not take time to add darkness to our lives, and Mrs. Grumpy is always down on something or someone. Of course, no one is ever glad to see Mrs. Grumpy; that is one of the reasons she *is* so grumpy. Choosing between, Mrs. Sunny and Mrs. Grumpy, guess who *needs* the greeting more. For, of course, Mrs. Sunny will be greeted by everyone; Mrs. Grumpy by almost no one. Mrs. Sunny's self-esteem is high; Mrs. Grumpy's is low to non-existent. Keep in mind, we have just sent Mrs. Grumpy a strong message that *she is not even worth a simple greeting.* As well, until someone helps Mrs. Grumpy begin to see herself as valuable, it would be foolish to expect her to change.

When a teacher greets his favorite class, he smiles, relaxes, and talks to many of them.   ("Hey, Jimmy, how are you doing? Melanie, you sound happy! New shoes, Kate?") But let the trouble-making, difficult class come along, and the greeting changes. ("Joe, get your hands away from her hair! Quiet, you're too noisy! Monica, don't push; wait your turn!") Yes, we tell them who they are to us and help shape who they will become. And once again, guess who needed us more.

We count and frequently begrudge every speck of attention and affection we give to the difficult children; yet, without ever counting it, we dispense far more time and energy to the easy, likeable children. When we are not greeting at reunion, we are acknowledging them throughout the day. We are sending messages to children all the time. Unfortunately and unhelpfully, we tend to interact differently with different types of children. I will never be called into a classroom to take a look at a charming child (Master Sunshine) who almost magically is given lots of attention, affection, and time. But I do get asked to help with a child (Miss Clouds) who gets these same items obnoxiously with temper tantrums, aggression, or inappropriate behavior. It is arresting that with some children we give away our affection and affirmation, and with other children we count everything they *steal*. Did we not choose to have children or to work with children to give away our affection, affirmations, and attention? Didn't we wish to make a positive difference in individual children's lives? Or only the easy, sunny ones? It takes a good deal of courage to face this last question.

It is Miss Clouds, the less socially skilled child with low self esteem, who needs us to make a positive difference in her life. She does not need fewer affirmations; she needs to be taught how to engender them. Master Sunshine needs less from us; his life is already great, and everyone else is busy trying to make it even better.

Further, we must get better at greeting and at affirming Existence at these wonderful opportunities. When we first see a child after school, many of us still ask, "What did you *do* today?" We have moved right into Accomplishments and completely overlooked Existence. And our children inevitably answer, "Nothing." If we are concerned about their behavior at school, we ask more invasively, "Were you good today?" or "Did you play nicely?" or "Did you hit anybody today?" or "Did you eat your lunch?" Not only are we off target, but what an opportunity we miss. We miss an opportunity to reconnect, to let them *know* how very important they are to us, to affirm their value in Existence. What if we simply gave them hugs and smiles and told them the truth, "I'm glad to see you!" As parents, we need to stop missing these daily opportunities which cement our relationship and our child's estimate of herself and her worth. What we say first to a child, our greeting, will be what they believe is most important. Which is more important? They exist still or they behaved well? If you have any difficulty with this answer, ask any parent who ever lost a child. These parents <u>know</u> the answer.

⌂ "Good morning."
> *Instead of:*
>> "It's time to get moving!"

⌂ "I'm so happy to see you. I missed you!" Big hug, big smile.
   Instead of:
      "Did any teacher have to talk to you today?"

⌂ "Welcome home. It's nice to have the family all together."

As teachers, we have the opportunity to help those children receiving little affirmation at home to improve their view of themselves and their own value.

🧍 "I'm glad you're here today, Scott. Welcome back, Julie."
   Instead of:
      "Put your coat on the hook."

🍎 "Hi, Kim, how's it going?"
   Instead of:
      "Did you do your homework?"

Parents remind me of how stressed and hurried they are when they pick up their children. Perhaps try a deep breath, a pause, and a reflection. You are about to see the person or persons whom you love most in the world. You likely either had them in pain or painfully worked through a bureaucracy to get them; they are the most important people in your life. And you get to see them. Surely, somewhere, you can find within a smile, a hug, and a "I'm glad to see you." If perchance you think your children do not notice how they are greeted, think again.

Greeting happens to be one of my stronger areas; I do tend to greet happily and affirm Existence. However, one day after school, I pulled up to pick up my son at middle school. I watched through the glass doors as he talked with his friends and talked with his friends and talked with his friends. Through elementary school, we parents tend to make the rules. In middle school, the children also begin to set rules for us. Now, I know the rules. The first rule is that parents may not do any uncool things, anything which might embarrass the child. Mothers do not go in to the school and fetch middle-schoolers. However, as time ticked away, I became increasingly irate. After a full five minutes, I decided to break the second rule; yes, I honked my horn. My son looked out for the first time, grabbed his stuff, and came quickly out to the car. I, of course, started my tirade-lecture (yes, this is a

Barrier to Cooperation), "Picking you up after school is a gift. I provide a service for you. There is absolutely no reason for me to lose five minutes of my time because you don't bother to look outside. My time may not seem valuable to you, but it is real important to me. Blah, blah, blah, blah, blah...." When I finally finished, there was a short pause; then my son grumbled, "So much for, 'Hi, Tim! Glad to see you. How was your day?'" They notice.

Teachers also share information. First, they are already too busy, and they do not have time to greet all of their students. One suggestion is to try 'targeting' students, especially, needy students. One technique is called the Two-Minute Intervention. For at least ten days, select one student to greet and converse with at the beginning or end of class, at recess, in the hall, or at lunch. Show interest and warmth to this student for one or two minutes per day. Watch your relationship change; watch the child bloom. Each of us has two minutes per day to give to a needy student.

The second point teachers make is that I have never met so-and-so; we'll call him Eric. Eric is described as a dreadful child, very, no, extremely difficult to like. Reportedly, no one likes Eric. We overlook that without the Eric's of this world, we would be less skillful teachers; for it is the difficult children who challenge us and keep us on our toes and keep us seeking and learning new information and skills. As well, many people could handle our jobs if only easy children were involved. It is the difficult children, the troubled children, the dysfunctional children, who require us to be skilled, trained, *professionals*. We are not making plates here; if a mistake is made with a plate, it becomes a second and sells for less. We cannot afford the luxury of seconds in our work. No child is a second. Although we get many chances with each child, in the end, we do not get another chance with youth and early formation of self-esteem and estimate of personal value. It is imperative that we maintain a high, professional level of skill when we work with children. The Eric's ensure that we do not slack off - not for a moment; with them in our room, we cannot. So the next time your difficult student appears at the door, you will be able to say in all sincerity:

"Hi, Eric, I'm glad to see you." And silently, remind yourself that if Eric weren't here, you might slack off and not do your best work today. And being an excellent teacher is truly important to you.

The hard truth is: Until you find a way to love him, he will be unable to find a way to love himself and begin his journey to "I am loveable."

We must also make sure we affirm Existence throughout the day, not only with greetings when we first meet. At home, bedtime, mealtime, and quiet times are great times for affirming. At preschool, nap time, lap time, line time, diaper time, and quiet times are available. For schools, recess, breaks, individual work time, passing periods, and individual tutoring times work. For our own children, smiles, hugs, hair ruffling, and pats play an important role. Teachers now must be aware of how they touch children and its ramifications and of who hates to be touched. Male teachers must be even more careful. However, smiles and affirming words are available to everyone.

Life Lesson

Our first words tell others what we believe are the most important issues or attributes. Greetings, though short, speak volumes.

Life Message

I am valuable to someone else. Others are glad to see me. I am likeable.

Take Time

Take time to <u>be</u> together.
Take time to listen to their thoughts, concerns, and interests.
Take time for play and fun.

Why is this strategy, this "time thing" as my friend Shauna calls it, so difficult to accomplish? Most likely because we have so little time. Dolores Curran in her eye-opening book *Traits of a Healthy Family* notes that:

"Lack of time, then might be the most pervasive enemy the healthy family has."

I agree completely. Each year seems to bring more and more busy-ness to families. More insidious, each year brings more acceptance of this fast-paced, stressful lifestyle. We are becoming increasingly desensitized to this pace and to the stress which inevitably accompanies it.

An acquaintance recently returned from a trip to England where afternoon tea is a daily ritual, where the pace is, as she described, civilized and healthy. She wants to return. It made such complete sense. I have been fortunate to spend a week in Mexico with women friends - all mothers. Although we enjoy the beach, the mountains, and the quiet reading times, without exception, our favorite part of the day is sunset. It has grown into an inviolate ritual - margaritas on the porch which overlooks the sea and faces the setting sun. Perhaps surprisingly, it is not the margaritas which are important. It is the pause, the time for each other and for our souls which we cherish. What grabs us is the contrast to 6:00pm at home where we are racing around chauffeuring children, trying to get done what we did not find time for earlier, and throwing together dinner. Again, here is a ritual of a guaranteed, calm, soothing time in the afternoon. Interestingly, what to some cultures is expected (long, relaxing lunch in France, tea time each afternoon in England) is considered unnecessary or sinful here in the United States.

Another friend, Jenny, arranges to sit with a cup of tea or coffee when her children arrive home from school. She looks forward to this little break. She is calm and focused as her children sit down with her and reconnect and talk about their day. Where is it written, "Thou shalt take no time for yourself or your family. No time for peace, solace, rejuvenation."

Do you sympathize with these feelings: a continual sense of hurry and urgency, a lack of control due in part to too little time to get everything done, a perception that time is getting away from you, and a longing for a simpler life? The expectations we have allowed ourselves and society to place upon us have raised our stress levels and stretched the fabric of our beings and families to drastic, unhealthy levels. Yet, most men continue to be trapped by the job status + money + power = your value myth, while most women are caught by the 'you can have it all' fantasy (as opposed to the more truthful 'you must *do* it all'). More and more, in order to be a good parent, it is expected that our children take numerous lessons, participate on sports teams, and be organization members; in short, they must fill every waking moment with all-important structure. *We have included and indoctrinated our children in our crazy pace!* No pause, no relaxing, no time off for good behavior - no time off period. All too often the very organizations which strive to strengthen families (church, scouts, volunteer organizations) actually become part of the time stealers. We do not have time to *be* a family; we are too busy *doing.*

Yes, we must learn to prioritize our time; but more importantly, we must limit our activities and expectations, carefully select personal and family activities, and set our personal values for our own and our family's time. We must no longer buy into the myth that the more involved a family the healthier it is. I now sometimes catch myself wondering why an extremely involved family *needs* to be so involved and when it finds time for itself and for regrouping, rejuvenating, relaxing, and rebonding. I wonder to myself, how do they manage? And at what cost? Dolores Curran reports that the 551 professionals she surveyed reported definitively that "the healthy family spends more time *together,* and not more time involved in activities that steal members from one another." The shift to less involvement and more family time has begun. Not only professionals, but families as well, are beginning to recognize the family's need for time together. As a family we must turn to our own structure and members for affirmation, support, healing, renewal, and meaning.

Perhaps we need to listen to Nobel prize winner, Mother Teresa's words:

I think the world today is upside-down, and is suffering so much, because there is so very little love in the homes and in family life. We have no time for our children, we have no time for each other; there is no time to enjoy each other.

This author would most respectfully add so very little love *demonstrated* in the homes and in family life. Love is not just a feeling; it is actions; it is how we treat someone. In order to be able to take time, many will first have to make time.

Of course, necessary to this time together is the development of a sense of humor and play, an ability to select activities fair to all, and the capability to treat one another with dignity and respect. Not to worry, these skills help us tremendously outside the family as well and are certainly worth the effort.

• Take time to be together

Have you ever experienced being with someone who, although is physically present, clearly is not there: a spouse watching a football game, a parent preparing dinner, a child playing video games? It is not enough to be present physically; we must learn to be present emotionally, to be available, to be tuned in to what is happening to others. Each of us carries our own duties, interests, concerns, and stresses; it can be difficult to move out of our own space and move into another's. Still it is critical that we take time to be there for each other.

• Take time to listen

Listening is one of the most important and recognizable ways that we connect with one another. Real listening takes place in the other's time frame and is rarely convenient or planned. It also involves his topics, interests, or concerns; too easily we transform the conversation to ours. Paradigm shift as a communication tool is the most sophisticated and powerful form of listening. Truly, it is the last parenting or dealing-with-people skill I would ever give up both personally and professionally. It is too important and too helpful to miss. It is the tool with which I have in fact built and maintained communication with my husband and my children. It gets me out of difficult situations with grace, dignity, and speed. Specifically, paradigm shift as a communication tool, reduces emotion, increases genuine communication, builds trust, credibility, bonds, and understanding, and gets to and through problems faster than any other skill. Paradigm shift as a communication skill is available on the third program of the Discipline For Life - One Step at a Time parenting audio series or in the teacher training audio or video programs.[11] It is a tool worth spending time developing.

If you have never spent time communing - just spending time in front of the fire place or on the back porch talking about anything and everything and nothing - with one of your children, you have missed some very special moments and some easy closeness and bonding which ease the tough times.

⌂ Take a walk with a child, daytime or nighttime, and make special memories for both of you.

⌂ Play golf or go fishing with a child. Where else can you find so much concentrated time together.

⌂ Take one child to lunch or dinner or weekend breakfast.

⌂ Leave extra, padded time each night to tuck them in, be together, and talk.

⌂ Schedule time with each of your children each week.

🕴 Early childhood teachers can use snack time, nap time, play time to *be* with and listen to an individual child.

🍎 Teachers can use recess, lunch, passing periods, extra curricular organizations, coaching time, and after school time. If you are a coach or organization sponsor, you have additional time with specific groups of students.

• Take time for play and fun

Some of us have a gift for creating fun; some of us do not. If you have difficulty finding fun or play activities, you might want to try one of the numerous books which give dozens to hundreds of ideas on fun activities for grown-ups and children to share. After all, if we do not manage to enjoy our children, why did we have them? The planet does not need a larger population, and few of us still need help bringing in the crops. Pleasure, fun, *joie de vivre* - joy in living is a need we all share. No matter who we are, there will likely be more than enough dark times. It is part of our job as humans to help create moments of delight, enchantment, fun, joy, merriment, and happiness. What else are we going to remember when we are old?

⌂ Read a longer 'chapter' book with your school-age child.

⌂ Shop together. Simply browse and share ideas; spending money is not necessary.

⌂ Play basketball together (no coaching), throw a ball back and forth (no tips).

⌂ Plant something together.

⌂ Cook or bake together.

⌂ Watch their television program and discuss it afterward.

⌂ Make something (craft, sewing, hobby) together. Remember whose project it is.

⌂ Play cards, checkers, chess, board games.

⌂ Create and build traditions - holiday, weekly, personal, bedtime, weekend.

⌂ Every now and again, simply live in the moment.

⌂ Laugh - it is good for you!

Early childhood teachers create fun frequently and well.
⚐ Join into their games and activities.

⚐ Talk and laugh during diaper changing.

⚐ Seat them next to you and in your lap.

⚐ Laugh with them; young children can be very funny.

Teachers of older children also have opportunities.
⚑ Go to physical education, music, or art class with them. Participate!

- Take field trips.

- Do fun class projects. (Use solar heat to cook hot dogs; there are books with many ideas.)

- Physically help with decorating. (No ideas needed, thank you!!)

- Remember that it is alright to laugh while teaching. Children are funny if our eyes are open to it.

- Learn to laugh at yourself.

Life Lesson

Time spent together can be our most precious gift and legacy.

Fun and laughter can be healthy.

Celebrate

Celebrate rather than reward. Show them with actions how much you value them.

Sometimes it is my children who teach me. Neither of my children enjoys homework; neither goes lightly to the task. But when my sons first started doing homework, I would occasionally take them a cold drink and snack while they were working. I always received thank you's and big smiles, and I knew in my head that this small act was appreciated. But it was not until the day when one of my sons brought me a cold drink while I was working in my office that I understood in my heart what these small gestures can mean. When my son carried in that first cold drink, I not only smiled and said my thank you, I also felt somewhere deep in my heart that someone really loved me, someone cared, someone cared enough to *do* something for me -to make my life easier and sweeter. This simple act touched my heart. Little things do count! As well, children love when we do a chore for them - especially if they are pressed for time, tired, or not feeling great. Anyone who has ever been ill, knows how good it feels when someone takes care of us in any way. Appreciation and love run deep. Whenever we do something for another without looking at what is in it for us, two of us feel better about ourselves.

There is a recent grass roots, ground-swell movement that sums up this concept nicely: *Practice random acts of kindness.* You may be amazed to discover how these small acts change attitude, emotional state, and character.

What is meant by celebrate rather than reward? Earlier we looked at the dangers of rewarding children, of linking rewards to behavior. However, I would hate to live in a world with no frills, no bonuses - without special things. We need only to remove the contingency of good behavior to change rewards into celebrations. The good things do not need to be linked to actions or accomplishments. Just hand out the bonuses sometimes in celebration. Of what? Of the fact that we are a family or a classroom, of the fact that time has passed, of Spring, of Winter, of Friday, of Monday, of good times, of moving through bad times, of nothing, of life.

At the end of each grading period, take the family out to dinner to celebrate having made it through yet another six weeks. Generally, one week later the report cards will arrive. Going to dinner is not contingent upon - did not depend upon - good grades. Every member of the family goes. This is a celebration, not a reward.

"Get out of trouble" coupons come in handy for both children and adults. I give them for birthdays and just every now and again for no reason. There are also "get out of a chore" coupons which are great for the children, less so for you since you will be doing the chore.

At preschool, young children love stamps, stickers, and stars. I would never want to take these precious items out of their lives. However, giving them only to the "good" children is not helpful; it discourages some, and teaches flawed principles. Instead, give them out as the children come through the door - to celebrate their arrival and to affirm Existence. Or give them out after nap time to celebrate another welcome back and return.

With elementary children in the classroom, place the box of stars on your desk and let each child decide if he wants to put one on his paper. The child who believes his paper is wonderful will take one and so will the child who is sad today or did not do great work. One of these children needed the star more; guess which one. Usually it is the one who, before, did not receive one. This child needs his existence affirmed. He needs to believe he has value regardless of his current level of accomplishment.

For older students at the beginning of the grading period, hand out "A" coupons or "No Homework" coupons which turn a failed paper or missing paper into a 100. Even high school students love bonuses. We never get too old to celebrate.

Life Lessons

Responsiveness is learned. Doing for others feels good and strengthens our bonds.

There is much more in life to celebrate than success.

Celebrations are fun regardless of what is celebrated. Fun is important.

Find and Acknowledge Each Child's Uniqueness

Each child is truly unique. As parents and as teachers, we must learn to appreciate each child as an individual. From color of hair or eyes or a smile like Grandpa's, from determination (stubbornness!) to easy-going, from practical to idealistic to creative, from filled with joy to filled with too much sorrow, from born old to forever young, from gifted to uncoordinated, from polished to rough-edged, from dependable to care-free, there are so many ways to see uniqueness and distinctiveness. Each of us wants to be understood and wants to be liked and accepted as we are. (How many relationships have failed because one party could not change the other?) We need to make sure we know the characteristics of our own children and the children in our classrooms. Each of us wants and needs to be special to someone. And we want to be liked and accepted as we are...warts and all.

Life Lesson

One of the more important yet most difficult traits we ever develop is tolerance.

Life Message

I am somebody. I am special. I am valuable.

At home, we have special nicknames for our loved ones; most of which we do not use in public. But we only take time to select affectionate nicknames for people we love. These, too, help us to build our bonds and to affirm uniqueness and value. Using nicknames or special names can also help us bond with our children. Most of us have a name used only by family members and close friends; sometimes it is a name never used in public. My closest friend in high school and I still instantly identify each other on the phone by nicknames used only between us. She lives far away, and I do not see her enough, but she will always be special to me. I know because only she calls me --- well, never mind. My husband rarely uses my full formal name except in public when he is calling me across a crowded room. At school, coaches most often use nicknames.

☞ Nicknames must not be put-downs. Only affectionate names are included.

☞ As your children get older, *never* use family nicknames in public! As children age so should their nicknames.

Life Lesson

With a few people, we have a very special, very strong bond. These are the important relationships in our lives.

Teach

Ask questions. Educate them on their own value.

Be clear with children. Tell them more than that you love them and care about them. Help them understand how and why you value and love them. Students also need this type of guidance from teachers. When a child seems to believe his value is dependent upon accomplishments, disrupt this belief system.

⌂ When they drop the ball in center field and when they catch it, ask: "Do I love you more when you catch the ball or when you drop it?"
⌂ "Do I love you more when you get A's or C's on your report card?"
⌂ "Do I love you more when you behave or when you don't?"

The correct answer: "Neither, it doesn't matter. I love you the same either way. I always love you."

⌂ "What's the difference between winning and losing?"
⌂ "What's the difference between getting a first place ribbon and a third place ribbon or getting no ribbon at all?"

The correct answer: "Winning's more fun."

⌂ "If I could choose from all the children in the world, who would I want to be my child?"

The correct answer: "YOU!" If they ask why: "Because you're you. Because we belong together. Because we are a family. Because I'm your Mom and you're my daughter."

♣ "Do I like you more when you behave or when you misbehave?"
🍎 "Do I like you more when you do good work or poor work?"

The correct answer: "Neither, it doesn't matter. I care about you just the same. You're always important to me. You are valuable either way."

🍎 "If I could choose from all the children (or classes in the world), who would I choose to have in my classroom this year?"

The correct answer: "You and you and you..." until you have included them all.   OR   "I would choose this exact class, just like it is."   As children get older and wiser, change the questions from "Do I...." to the even more important "Do you believe you have more value...."

Telling your child you love him but do not like him can be hurtful and dangerous. Our children not only need to be loved, they need to be liked. How can I be loveable and not likeable is a question children cannot answer, nor can I. Quite frankly, we each want to be likeable, not just loveable. Too many of us have relatives we love (because we have to or are supposed to) but whom we do not like. We really only want to spend time with those we like and enjoy. Check your own really good friends; you love them and you like them. Our children want and need both.

Try:
   "I do not wish to be with you right now. I need some space for myself."
   OR   An appropriate discipline technique to change the undesirable behavior.   OR   DESCRIPTIVE CRITICISM (See DESCRIPTIVE CRITICISM in Mistakes Chapter of this Section.)
Instead of:
   "I love you, but I don't like you."

When we further discuss criticism, we will learn how confusing and dangerous to self-discipline the concept, "I like you, but I don't like your behavior" is. However, most of us have been taught this "Separate the deed from the doer." Using Descriptive Criticism will get us entirely out of this bind.

Life Lesson

I have value simply because I exist.

Most Precious Gifts

These are love, time, understanding, and an unwavering belief in each child.

What more does anyone need emotionally?

If you love me, you give me time freely and make sure you have time for me. If you give me time, you will come to understand me. And if you understand me, you will believe in me.

• One Key to Encouragement:

We are frequently told we must be encouraging; yet it continues to be difficult to know exactly how to accomplish this. One important key is unwavering belief. Hopefully, each of us has had at least one person in our lives who has always *believed* in us, who becomes a touchstone for us. Unwavering belief is deeply encouraging.

Periodically in the growing years, a child may meet someone whose confidence in her abilities will not only surprise her, but will have a profound impact upon how she views herself and her ability to tackle new challenges. Here is a story about the gift a very special camp counsellor gave a young and frightened child.

At age nine, Vicky, previously a competent swimmer, had a near drowning experience in a pool. Not unexpectedly, her confidence in her ability to survive, let alone enjoy, water play vanished. The following year she attended a summer camp where swimming was a daily event, indeed a requirement for many of the things she wanted and loved to do. Fear, anxiety, and disappointment became her constant companions. In order to paddle a canoe, her greatest passion in life, Vicky had to swim 200 yards. She was convinced that she could not meet this requirement: she could not swim 200 yards. She told them so with conviction.

There was, however, a young waterfront counsellor, named Kim, who believed that things were not so bleak. Over a period of several days, she took on Vicky's fears and anxieties in what was a difficult battle. Each time

Vicky refused to try and insisted she could not swim, Kim would calmly and gently reaffirm her belief that Vicky could. Furthermore, Kim added, she was prepared to help at any time. Finally, a compromise was struck. With Kim's continual but quite insistence, Vicky got into the water with Kim at her side coaching her through what seemed the most perilous 200 yard journey of her life. You are probably not at all surprised to discover that this swimming episode was ultimately successful. Despite a few momentary panics, Kim's patience and belief that this child could conquer this challenge prevailed.

Seven years later, Vicky was herself a qualified lifeguard and had long since forgotten how scary the water had once been. It was not until much later that she realized that in the darkness of those days when she had felt helpless, stupid, and terrified, Kim's unwavering belief had been a beacon of light. Kim's gentle and reassuring manner had made all the difference. Years later, as a parent, Vicky would marvel at the wisdom of this young university student and be thankful for her priceless gift.

Trait: Positiveness

A final note on the positiveness which accompanies self-esteem firmly built in this area of Existence. Generally these children are recognizable on sight. They include the new child in the neighborhood or in the classroom who arrives and before she has ever spoken a word, her entire body language says, "Hi, you'll like me!" And you know what, you will, starting right now. These children and adults are easy to like. They have found another key:

If I like me, you will like me. And if you like me, I will like me even more. And on and on and on.

Of course, sadly but inevitably, the reverse is true as well:

If I am not sure I like me, you probably won't like me much. And if you do not like me much, I will begin to like myself less. And on and on and on.

We help determine which spiral they will travel and become.

Self-esteem built on Existence is the most stable; it is value we can depend on to be there for us regardless of circumstance or fortune. It is also the foundation for building self esteem in the other two areas. Every child and every adult requires an understanding and certainty of his own worth.

Self-esteem based on existence is a requisite for emotional health.

13:
Accomplishment

LIFE MESSAGE: I Can Think and Do For Myself - I am Capable
TRAIT: Confidence

Earlier, we looked carefully at the relative importance of each of the areas of self-esteem. This second area was determined to be the least important as well as the most problematic. It too often becomes the center for all self-esteem and thereby weakens the foundational area of Existence, and destroys the quick-improvement area of Mistakes. We determined that too much investment in this area is not only detrimental to the other more important areas' development but also dangerous to the individual. We also looked at how precarious and unsteady self-esteem built in this area is, and how vulnerable it is to quick collapse. We must also keep in mind that most of the skills we have been taught that affirm self-esteem concentrate on this area.

We have all heard that "Nothing succeeds like success." Undeniably, we all know that we feel better about ourselves when we succeed or accomplish. Even though this is the weakest domain of self-esteem, it is, nevertheless, one of the areas. With a final caution to keep from over-recognizing and over-affirming this area, let us look at ways to build self-esteem helpfully in this second category of self worth.

Praise or Descriptive Appreciation[12]

It seems everyone has heard of praise and is aware that praising children is important. Most of us were taught that good parents or teachers praise children; better parents or teachers praise even more. Yet, as with most communication skills, improvement can be made and needs to be made. Our concepts need to be re-thought. Communication skills (discipline and dealing with people skills included) are not unlike technology. We start with an idea, and we work with it for a while, and then we make improvements and remove the *bugs*. Not so long ago, we had to go through an operator to phone our neighbor. Today we can call on a mobile phone, send a fax, or leave a message on an answering machine. The bugs are out and improvements have been made. Many communication skills have benefitted from improvements through time. It is time to review praise.

Originally, the use of praise was encouraged because we understood that everyone enjoys *occasional* acknowledgment of jobs well done. Further, it was recognized that saying something positive to a child was better than saying only negatives - especially if we are not skilled at helpful criticism. Even more importantly, it was recognized that saying something positive to a child was far superior to saying nothing at all. Too many children were receiving no positive acknowledgment. Neither negativity nor lack of acknowledgment helped self-esteem. However, praise, like almost every communication skill, had some rough edges that can indeed use some smoothing. It is time to tackle the fine tuning of praise. First, let us locate the *bugs*.

Several concerns about praise, as it has traditionally been taught, have surfaced over the last several years. Praise is often used as verbal reinforcement. Many of the concerns discussed earlier which apply to reinforcement in general also apply to this verbal reinforcement. It can be manipulative; most of us were taught that one of the reasons to praise behavior is to get a child to repeat the desired behavior. This is manipulation. During live seminars, I have asked thousands of participants to raise their hands if they enjoy being manipulated by others. No one ever raises a hand. Next I ask them to raise their hand if they believe and teach the Golden Rule, "Do unto others as you would have them do unto you." Everyone raises their hands. And each is trapped by her own integrity. Why? Because if we practice what we teach and believe, we treat others as we wish to be treated and do not treat them in ways we do not wish to be treated. We are no longer free to manipulate anyone, because we, ourselves, do not like to be manipulated.

Another concern is that we have been taught that praise must take place immediately to be effective and, thus, involves immediate gratification. Deferred gratification, the ability to wait for what we want, patience, is a truly helpful principle and virtue. As well, praise is externally motivating rather than internally motivating. Intrinsic motivation carries far greater strength than extrinsic motivation. We need children and adults who are self-motivating. Through such external motivation, children tend to become dependent upon praise. This praise dependence is a problem for many children since they ultimately need more and more praise. One teacher described her class as praise junkies. When a student answers a question in class and the teacher does not respond with, "Yes," "Good," or "That's right," many pupils do not know what to do or think - even when they were quite sure their answer was correct. This leads us to children failing to develop a sense of evaluation. As with internal motivation, it is ability to evaluate internally that is critical. Democracies require voters who can evaluate and judge ideas, issues, and candidates; without voters with these skills a democracy is destined to founder. Deferred gratification, internal motivation, and evaluation are signs of growing maturity, self-discipline, and initiative.

An additional concern involves our credibility. Praise, at times, may lack sincerity and believability, partly because we strive to give so much praise so often, and partly because we try to give praise to all children and leave no one out. Interestingly, the more superlative we become, the less believable our praise becomes. We give praise so often that our children or students sometimes tune us out. Our credibility is called into question. For example, every now and again my husband and I decide to go out to dinner - *alone* - without the children so that we can remember why we got married in the first place. I am no fool. I look differently from what I did twenty years ago, and truthfully, although I am getting better, I look no better. And there are women out there right now who look like I did twenty years ago; actually some of them have looks I never came close to ever. So, when my husband asks me out to dinner, I go into our bathroom and do things to my face and hair - improvements. When I finish, I look in the mirror to see how I have done. One of two things happens. Sometimes, and young women out there take heed, I see my mother. This is not good. Not by any means because my mother is ugly, but because she is old. She has *always* been old. Even when she was younger than I am now. (Everything is relative. Isn't your mother old?) About this time my husband comes back to see if I am ready. When he looks at me, he realizes I have worked on myself. Now he would tell you himself that he has a great deal invested in me and that he, too, is no fool. So, of course, he says, "Honey, you look great. Are you ready to go?" Now I have just looked in the mirror and seen my mother, his mother-in-law. There are only three questions I can ask myself: *Does he need new glasses again?* We just did that. *Has he lost his "eye" for women?* I doubt it. *Is his credibility or believability high?* No.

The reality is that sometimes the second option occurs when I look in the mirror. I realize I look about as good as I am ever going to again. I see me, not my mother. This is good. My husband shows up about now and says - exactly the same thing, "Honey, you look great. Are you ready to go?" I love him dearly, but he knows, as do we all, what he is *supposed* to say. And credibility weakens because of this knowledge. Children recognize this factor as well. Our credibility is too important to be compromised.

Another group of concerns about praise centers on the second reason we were taught to praise - to build self-esteem. This purpose, too, needs to be re-examined. It is possible that praise has caused more harm to self-esteem than benefit in the last several years. I realize that this is a very radical statement. But if you begin to consider that there are three areas of self-esteem requiring affirmation and that praise addresses only the weakest area (Accomplishments), compromises the quick-improvement area (Mistakes), and ignores the most important (Existence), the idea gains strength. Further, for many of us, praise is the only tool we have been taught to use to build self-esteem. As a result, too many children and adults have self-esteem built solely or largely on accomplishments. Dependent upon unreliable, receding successes, self-esteem is shaky, erratic, and vulnerable. Lastly, when we see self-esteem falter in these children, we work hard to help them rebuild it - *using praise as the major tool, we end up in exactly the same bind and jeopardy!*

One of these problems with praise, that of self-esteem being built exclusively in the area of Accomplishments, must be addressed by learning numerous affirming skills in the areas of Existence and Mistakes. We must affirm these areas much more often.

These concerns notwithstanding, we must still cope with manipulation, lack of evaluation skills, and praise dependence. These obstacles can best be overcome by fine tuning our praise, improving it, and removing these bugs. Clearly, we will need to take out the evaluative aspect of praise, and we will need to find a way to avoid manipulation. The result is sometimes called descriptive appreciation; if you are more comfortable with the old term, you can easily continue to think of this skill as altered praise or improved praise. Descriptive appreciation differs from traditional praise in two important aspects.

First, it is descriptive only. No evaluation is involved; by contrast, traditional praise evaluates: Great! Terrific! Good Girl! I know some of you have one of those posters which give 100 ways to say 'good' to your child. This concept of varying the way we say good is not nearly so helpful as descriptive appreciation. One hundred different ways to say 'good' addressed only that we sounded canned and repetitive. It did not address praise dependence or external evaluation. What we say to a child about her (external evaluation) is not nearly so important as what she says to herself (internal evaluation) about who she is or what she has done. Descriptive appreciation is more powerful and empowering and runs much more deeply into the child's evaluation of herself.

Second, it is important that we change our intent from manipulation to expressing appreciation. When we manipulate, we teach and will reap manipulation. When we express appreciation, we teach responsiveness - the ability to respond empathetically to other people's feelings and needs. Responsiveness is a wonderful trait to develop in either child or adult. The roots of the term descriptive appreciation are clear.

To illustrate descriptive appreciation it is helpful to compare it to praise as originally taught. For example, a daughter has decided to knit golf club covers as a gift for her father's birthday. Any father who opens a hand-made birthday, or any birthday gift for that matter, knows he must respond. Praise is the response that tends to come to mind, "They're beautiful! Just what I needed. Terrific."

"Do you really like them?" asks his daughter. It is easy to understand how a child who has never before knit anything so complicated or given so much of herself in a gift might feel unsure of herself and her gift.

"Yes, they're wonderful - perfect!" To reassure her, father gets even more superlative, probably decreasing his credibility and increasing her doubt. Evaluations (beautiful, terrific, wonderful, perfect) often lack credibility and, hence, may be perceived as less than genuine.

On the other hand, using descriptive appreciation, father may instead say, "These covers must have taken you hours and hours to knit. They're made of sturdy yarn; they'll protect my golf clubs. And they are the same color as my golf bag. Thank you for helping me celebrate my birthday."

"You're welcome," she replies, comfortable in the knowledge that he does like her gift, and more importantly, that she made a great birthday present. She says to herself, "I did it; I am a great knitter; I give great gifts; I helped my dad celebrate his birthday." Descriptions are difficult to dismiss; they evoke believability. How we employ descriptive appreciation follows.

Two Steps To Descriptive Appreciation
1. Describe what you see or what has been done that you appreciate.
2. Allow the child to evaluate for himself.

Here are some examples.

To the child who has cleaned up his room.
Try saying:
> "You put your books all on the shelf and your dirty clothes in the hamper. I can't find a single toy on the floor. And every corner of your comforter is off the floor - just like the policy says. It is a pleasure for me to walk in here."
> *Child may say to himself:* "I did it! I can clean my room. I did a great job!"

Instead of:
> "Your room looks terrific."
> *Child may say to himself:* "I hope she doesn't find the clean clothes stuffed in the drawer."

Instead of:
   "You did a great job picking up your room."
   Child may say to himself: "You made me do it. I didn't want to."

Instead of:
   "Your desk is still a mess."
   Child may say to himself: "Nothing is ever good enough."

⌂ To the child who has just given you a handmade potholder:
Try saying:
   "You chose thick, thick quilted material for this potholder; it will protect my
      hand no matter how hot the pan is. It covers my whole hand. And
      it matches the colors in the kitchen. It is a wonderful feeling knowing
      you spent so much of your time to make me a gift to celebrate my
      birthday. Thanks, darlin'."
   Child may say to herself: "She likes it!" (least important) "I make terrific
      potholders, and I helped my mom celebrate her birthday. I help
      create happiness." (more important)
Instead of:
   "This is so beautiful! I love it! You're so sweet to make me a present."
   Child may say to herself: "I wonder if she really likes it." OR "Dad said
      I had to make you something."

⌂ To the child who has managed not to be ugly to his pestering baby sister.
Try saying:
   "You have been trying to play with your blocks for fifteen minutes.
      You've given your sister a few blocks for herself, and you've gotten
      her favorite stuffed animal to distract her. You even moved your
      blocks to the table where she can't knock them down. And you've
      talked to her nicely every time. Not every big brother can handle a
      situation like this."
   Child may say to himself: "I treat people nicely; I am nice. I am a good
      big brother. I can solve problems."
Instead of:
   "You've been such a good big brother. I'm so proud of you."
   Child may say to himself: "I'm not such a good brother; I'm just about
      ready to push her down and out of the way. I'm tired of her."

⌂ To the sixteen year old who has returned home on time.
Try saying:
"You win; you beat the curfew!"
Child may say to himself: "Just by a few seconds, but I did it."

"I'm glad to see you," is also an excellent alternative but not an example of this section's descriptive appreciation.

Instead of:
"You are so trustworthy!"
Child may say to himself: "If you only knew what we've been doing, you wouldn't say that. But you don't know."

Instead of:
"You're lucky - this time. Make sure you get here next time or, I mean it, you'll be grounded."
Child may say to himself: "Yeah, right, whatever."

♟ To the young child who asks if you like her picture or if her picture is good.
Try saying:
"There is lots of bright green; it makes me feel like I want to go outside in the Spring time."
Child may say to himself: "She likes it." (least important) "I'm a good artist; I make terrific pictures!" (more important)

Instead of:
"It's beautiful; I love it."
Child may say to himself: "She says that to everybody." OR "I hate it; I couldn't make the bunny look like a bunny; it looks like a man, not an animal."

"What do you like about it?" or "Tell me about your picture; it looks like you spent some time on this." These are, of course, also appropriate responses, but not examples of this section's descriptive appreciation.

♣ To the young children who have just finished cleaning up all the play areas before snack time.

Try saying:
> "Just look at our room. Every one of the big blocks is on the shelf; the crayons are all in their baskets. The books are standing in the bookcase where they belong, and the modeling clay is safely zipped up in the plastic bags. It feels good to look around and see so many things back in their place. I feel lucky to be a member of this class. We are ready for snacks."

> *The children may say to themselves:* "We did it! Our room is all picked up. We are ready for snack time." OR "I picked up lots of blocks. I contributed. I am part of this class. I'm glad I'm in this class." OR "Jenny and I picked up the crayons. We did a great job."

Instead of:
> "You all did an excellent job!" "This room looks great."

> *The children may say to themselves:* "I didn't do anything - again." OR "I just threw a couple of crayons in the basket." OR "There are a bunch of crayons under the piano bench that you haven't noticed. I don't think now is the time to tell you."

● To the child whose work paper is one of the finest she has ever done.

Try saying: *(or writing on paper)*
> "You used capital letters to start your sentences and periods to end them. You found places for three paragraphs, and your printing was very easy to read. You must be very happy with this paper and yourself."

> *Child says to herself:* "I can do good work!" OR "It was worth the effort; I'm glad I worked hard." OR "I understand sentences - finally!"

Instead of:
> "Good work!" "Terrific paper!"

> *Child says to herself:* "I wish I knew what I did on this paper that makes it different from the others."

Instead of:
> "It's about time. I knew you could do it!" (back-handed compliment)

> *Child says to herself:* "Thanks," said weakly, with rolled eyes.

🍎 To the class who has continued working quietly while you talked to a parent or the principal in the hall.

Try saying:
"It is wonderful to realize I can be away from you, and you can keep working and stay quiet by yourselves. That's what self-discipline and responsibility are all about. Thank you. I am proud to be your teacher." OR "Mrs. Stewart had some important things she needed to discuss with me. It was very nice for me to be able to take time with her when she needed it and not have to worry about you. Thanks."

Class may say to themselves: "We can keep working. We are a good class." OR "I got most of my spelling done; I won't have to do it for homework." OR "I can work by myself. I am responsible. I am capable."

Instead of:
"You were so good while I was talking to Mrs. Stewart." OR "You are so responsible."

Class may say to themselves: "Aren't we good other times?" OR "Actually, I was writing notes to Becky."

Life Lesson

Children learn to evaluate for themselves and to pat themselves on the back.

Life Messages

I am capable.
I like what I do; others like what I do.

These are the ways we can remedy praise without throwing the baby out with the bath water. If someone had asked you when you were first learning about praise: Would you rather teach children to look for a pat on the back for a job or deed well done, or how to pat themselves on the back and begin to learn for themselves how to evaluate?

I believe you would have chosen the latter.   Praise teaches the first; Descriptive Appreciation teaches the second.

• Proximity Praise
"I like the way Martha is sitting quietly."
"Will has *his* hands folded."

Many of us have been taught to use Proximity Praise. This is a strategy contrived to change mildly inappropriate behavior to more desirable behavior. For example, when Allison is not paying attention, we look at Jay who is sitting next to her and is attending and say, "I like the way you're paying attention, Jay." Three problems exist in this technique.

First, the phrasing "I like the way...." is weak and judgmental. Many students, especially as they get older, do not really care what we like; thus, this statement has little effect on them. In addition, the locus of judgment or evaluation is external not the more meaningful internal. Second, both phrasings involve a comparison - one of the Barriers to Cooperation discussed in the Gaining Cooperation section. When we compare children, we are more likely to generate resistance than cooperation, and we also create competition, rivalry, and strife among children.

The third problem is that we are talking to one child in order to send a message to a second child. This qualifies as something more than indirect; it is almost within the realm of dishonest, and at the very least faulty communication. Earlier, in the Section on Descriptive Language, we looked at the problems with indirect communication. When communication is this dramatically indirect, it is unhealthy. It is more honest, direct, fair, and helpful to speak to the child who needs the message. Put simply, *speak to the child you are addressing.* It makes more sense.

• "I'm proud of you"

Happily, parents and teachers often find themselves realizing that one of their children has done something wonderful, something to be proud of, something out of the ordinary. Almost instinctively, we all respond, "I'm so proud of you." And many of us believed those to be some of the sweetest words uttered to us. We wanted our parents, our teachers, or any adult we respected to be proud of us. It is again helpful to fine tune this phrase and remove a remaining concern.

I graduated from a small high school in my hometown. During my school years I rarely carried books home and rarely did homework (ask my friends). Book learning has always been easy for me. So it was with precious little effort, I managed to graduate with high academic standing. At graduation, many adults were kind enough to stop me and tell me how proud of me they were. Without question, they meant well. Even so, these remarks made me feel awkward. I was completely aware of how little effort I had exerted, especially compared to my friends. When someone would tell me how proud they were of me for my academic success, I always replied, "Thanks - I made the basketball team three years in a row." No one ever listened long or carefully enough to really hear me or grasp my point of view. I wanted to pass over the easy accomplishment about which I was not terribly proud or excited (academic success) and move to what I felt was the major accomplishment of which I was very proud and for which I had given great effort (basketball success). Six of us made the girls' basketball team our sophomore year; usually only two sophomores at most made it. The competition was stiff. I had worked hard and wanted with all of my heart to make that team. I still remember and appreciate the teacher who let me out of class to go check the just-posted list, and I still remember actually seeing my name. Academic success was important, and I was pleased about it. But making the basketball team my sophomore year and the two following years was my finest accomplishment. My point is that what I was proud of and what others were proud of were two different things. *And I was right!* It was my judgment, my evaluation which was most important; it is, after all, my life and my accomplishments.

The second thing I questioned was anyone else's right to be proud of me. Why were grown-ups, especially those who had contributed nothing to my academic success, proud of me? In my heart, I recognized that it was I who needed to be proud, that pride is in self, not in others. In the dictionary pride is defined as "a reasonable or justifiable <u>self</u>-respect" (emphasis added). I concur that pride is largely a feeling related to self, an internal evaluation. However, there is some room for confusion. The dictionary also defines pride as "a delight or elation arising from <u>some</u> act." (emphasis added). Notice it says some, not one's own, act. Perhaps it is fair game for someone else to be proud of us. Nevertheless, it is still important to remember that our pride in ourselves is more important than someone else's pride in us. With that in mind, we may want to take some opportunities to make the following modifications.

Consider changing,   "I am proud of you."
To: "I bet <u>you're</u> feeling proud."
    "You seem awfully happy (excited) about that!"
    "I'm proud to be your mom (teacher)."
    "I'm proud to know you (have you for a friend)."
    "I am so happy for you!" or "How exciting!"

A final note to teachers who continue to be evaluated with forms which include a segment on praise. Many evaluators cannot distinguish between praise and descriptive appreciation. When they can, your score will be higher for using descriptive appreciation. When they cannot, you will still do well. In fact, teachers have stated that their ratings went up when using descriptive appreciation. The evaluators may not perceive the difference, but they hear plenty of excellent praise going on in your classroom. The result is a high rating in the praise category.

Self-imposed Victims and Learned Helplessness

> Not being able to govern events, I govern myself. - Michael deMontaigne

Too many of us know people who do not direct their lives, who do not take responsibility for how they respond to what happens to them, and who do not choose their own paths. Each of us is open to two types of victimization. The first is perpetrated upon us; no one is safe from violation from the outside. Robbery, assault, rape, and abuse strike everywhere and any one. Although we can take safety precautions, this is not the type of victimization we can prevent completely, nor a type for which we are responsible. Nor is it the type of victimization addressed in this section. The second kind of victimization is that which we do to ourselves and involves the portions of our lives which we can control, which we are responsible for, but which we allow other people and even events to regulate. This victimization is self-made; the helplessness is a learned posture or response.

We are not in control of, nor are we responsible for, others' actions. We are, however, responsible for our own actions and for our own responses to others' actions and events which take place in our lives. It is here where we, ourselves, tolerate, permit, and even excuse victimization or helplessness.

It is when someone passively *allows* or even actively *encourages* others to control his life, or when by abnegation or surrendering of responsibility invites negative occurrences or abuse that signifies this second type of victim. It is when someone chooses to allow abuse to occur or chooses to flirt with dangerous outcomes or consequences that this type of victimization takes place. Too many of us know someone whose life seems to happen *to* them rather than their taking responsibility for it and choosing to direct it. This is the person who always has an excuse at the ready whenever anything goes wrong. *"I would have been on time for work this morning, but the alarm clock didn't ring."* (If you don't set it, it will not ring.) *"I would have gotten a better grade on my math test, but there was a great movie on television last night."* (Watching the movie happened to you?) *"The bartender never should have let me leave the bar that drunk. If he'd have stopped me, I wouldn't have wrecked my car."* (Who chose to drink and drive?)

> When you blame others, you give up your power to change.
> - unknown

As is evident by the parenthetical comments, I have what seems to be diminishing sympathy for those who would blame others or events for the condition of their lives. There are many different levels and types of victimization. Some forms of victimization may fall into both categories. The Children's Defense Fund reported in February, 1994, that in one day in

America, 2,781 teenagers became pregnant and 3,325 babies are born to unmarried women, and that 7,945 children are reported abused or neglected. These statistics include children victimized by others and children victimized secondarily or primarily by themselves. Some of those pregnancies were neither judicious nor premeditated choices. They were simply allowed to happen without effort to prevent them. Some of the abuse was repeated and might have been prevented *if, and only if, the child knows and is able to speak out to a different adult.* We must teach children to take back their lives. No child can be blamed for or held responsible for being abused; some children, however, have taken responsibility for stopping abuse.

It is one thing to be surrounded by a war about which you can do precious little or to be a young child being manipulated, frightened, and abused. It is another matter entirely to blame a movie for a poor test grade. I do have great empathy and immense concern when I see a child taking the *Victim Path.* ("No one will play with me on the playground."   "All of my friends are doing it." "I can't." "He told me to.") More importantly, I also see glaring, vital opportunities to teach children how not to be victims and how to help themselves away from this Victim Path, and how to avoid a lifestyle of learned helplessness.

A crucial part of our job as parents or teachers is to teach children how to own their lives, their choices and responses, and to avoid becoming victims to themselves and by their own lack of knowledge, skills, or understanding. Each of us needs to learn responsibility and life-recovery skills. Each of us must learn to own our life and when necessary, to take back our life. *It is up to each of us to NEVER allow victims to continue down the path of victimization and learned helplessness.*

The Children's Defense Fund has adopted as its motto, "Leave no child behind." This motto applies well to the Victim Path.

Picture the self-allowed victims that you know. Are they emotionally healthy or happy? Victims rarely are. As a graduate student, I remember reading a research study which I recall to this day as the "monkey in the sidecar" experiment.   Researchers were working with various pairs of monkeys trying to determine how intelligent and flexible they were. They placed one monkey in a little compartment (the control car) with a seat wired for mild electrical shock and with a panel in front with three buttons that could be lit up by the experimenters. They placed a second monkey in another compartment (the sidecar) separated from the first by a clear, plexiglass shield. This second compartment had no light-buttons on the panel; it did, however, have the same wired seat. Initially, the experiment sought to determine if monkeys were smart enough to figure out that when the light-buttons were turned on, an electrical shock followed in a few seconds. The lighted buttons served as a warning. Both monkeys were simultaneously administered the same mild shock. And indeed, the monkeys soon figured out the connection and showed signs of distress as soon as the lights came on. Further, the researchers wanted to know if the monkey in the control car would then try to turn off the light-buttons and prevent the shock. Yes, they did. Looking for more intelligence, the researchers changed the format and rules and subsequently required the monkey in the control car to turn the light-buttons off in a specific sequence in order to prevent the shock. The monkeys managed to adjust to this new development. When the sequence was changed, the monkey in the control car learned to try new sequences until he got it right and prevented the shock. Whenever the first monkey used the correct sequence, both monkeys avoided the electrical shock; when he missed, they both received the shock. After the monkey had mastered one sequence for a number of trials, the researchers would randomly change to a different correct sequence. The monkey, intelligent and flexible, would work to find this new sequence until he got it right and again avoided the electrical shock. The last twist of this experiment was that no sequence was correct. Regardless of what sequence the monkey tried, both were shocked. Then the researchers returned both monkeys to the large habitat area where all of the monkeys were kept.

It was at this juncture that the researchers discovered additional findings unrelated to intelligence, but associated with victimization. For very quickly, they found that they had to remove one member of each pair of monkeys from the monkey society for what they labeled as neurotic-like, aggressive, antisocial, violent behavior. Can you guess which set of monkeys needed isolation? It was the monkeys who had been in the sidecar, not the monkeys who had been in the control car. This outcome provides us with several very important inferences.

First, it was neither the problem, nor its negative outcome or punishment, the electrical shocks (equal to both sets), which caused the harmful changes. The significant variable was the ability to try to deal with the problem versus inability to try to solve the problem. I believe that the monkeys in the control car were just too busy to break down or to deteriorate emotionally. Some of us may feel this is one of the main factors helping us stay sane; we do not have the time for a nervous breakdown! It is the ability to take action or to have some control over our destiny that helps us cope in a healthy way. When that ability is taken away, when we become passive, helpless victims with no control over our fate, we become emotionally unhealthy. Thus, it is not the existence of a problem, but the lack of problem solving skills which disturbs us.

Second, this emotional distress is displayed in aggressive, antisocial, insensitive, callous behavior. We have known for years that many child abusers (both sexual and physical) were themselves victims of abuse. Helplessness or victimization too often brings about its reverse behavior. Those who had no control take control over someone else and perpetuate this ugly cycle. Those who were victimized become the perpetrators.

Lastly, we need to look at exactly what was needed to keep the first set of monkeys (in the control car) emotionally stable and non-violent. It is not, as so many of us believe, finding the solution to the problem. Solving the problem is not necessary to emotional health. Remember, in the final stages of the experiment, the monkeys could not and did not avoid the electrical shock. They left the situation having failed.

It is not *solving* a problem which is required for emotional health. It is *trying to solve* the problem which is necessary. We do not have to succeed; we only have to take some action, any action. If it is not the right action, we need only try again.

> God doesn't require us to succeed; He only requires that you
> try. - Mother Teresa

Thus, emotional health does not require a problem-free life nor continual success with problems. Emotional health requires only that we work on the problems, that we take control of our actions and responses, that we do not engage in or permit ourselves helplessness in any situation where we are not. How can we help children develop appropriate skills? Here are three ways.

• Notice children taking the Victim Path   Never allow them to continue. Helplessness must always be addressed.

We must make sure we understand and see incidents of self-imposed helplessness when they occur. We must be aware and notice this style of operating. It is very easy to miss, to ignore, or to rescue. We must be careful to avoid these.

• Change reactive language to proactive language

First, we must learn to recognize the early, innocuous signs of the Victim Path.   One of the earliest and clearest signals of victimization is our language. This pattern has often been described as Reactive Language (used by victims) and Proactive Language (used by healthy individuals). Reactive language comes from a belief that others determine our behavior and emotional state. From this viewpoint, we have little or no control over our lives. On the other hand, proactive language stems from taking responsibility for our decisions and actions and for the resulting consequences and from a sense of ownership of self. Remember, *I am responsible for what I choose to do and for what happens to me and others as a result of these decisions and actions.*   This belief is fundamental to maturity, self-discipline, responsibility, and any DISCIPLINE system.

Reactive Language	Proactive Language
I can't	I can
They won't let me	I am capable
I have to	I choose
If only	Let's change
They won't	I can influence others
She made me	I am responsible
It wasn't my fault	I did
He makes me so mad	I won't let him get to me,I control my feelings
I don't know why I did that	I am responsible for my choices
I would	I will
There's nothing we can do	We can figure out something
Others limit me	I limit myself and I set myself free
That's the way I am	I can change

Whenever you hear reactive language from a child, help him change to proactive. For example:

⌂ *Help change:*
"I can't get up this morning."
To:
"I stayed up late last night, and now I don't want to get up. I wish I didn't have to, but I do."

🏃 *Help change:*
"Joshua makes me so mad."
To:
"I don't like playing with Joshua; I think I'll play with Michael for a while."

🍎 *Help change:*
"If only the test hadn't been so hard, I could have gotten a better grade."
To:
"I chose to quit studying too soon, and I blew the test as a result."

• Teach problem-solving skills

     If there is no wind, row. - Latin proverb

Children tend to have child-size problems, whereas adults have larger, adult-size problems. Of course, we hope adults also have greater skills. In order to develop these better problem-solving skills, we need opportunities to learn and practice small skills on small problems.

Every problem offers an opportunity for strengthening old abilities or learning and developing new problem-solving skills.

Work with children on their actual problems. These problems provide wonderful teaching opportunities. When a young child comes to me and says, "No one will play with me on the playground," a red flag for helplessness instantly rises. Here is an example of our conversation and an opportunity to teach.

"No one will play with me on the playground. They never let me."

"That must hurt very much."

"Yes, I hate it."

"It's difficult to be out there thinking no one wants to play."

"I want to be part of the group; I want them to let me play."

"Would you like to know some things other children have done to get children to play with them?"

"Yes!"

Notice that I did not say, "Here's what you should do." Advice says I am smart and can solve problems, and you are not and cannot. Nor is it generally helpful to say, "It's your problem, sweetheart." Abandonment says I don't care, and I will not help you. Nor, "I'll play with you." To have the solution given teaches "rescue, rescue, rescue"; look to someone else to rescue you; other people solve your problems. Too often we confuse nurturing, which means to further development or to educate, with rescuing and removing obstacles and problems as quickly as possible.

I now have this child in the palm of my hand - to teach. It is time to ask her what options she can think of and to offer several alternatives. The alternatives may depend to a certain extent on our knowledge of this particular child and her specific hurdles. Always make sure to give several choices; it is important that the child makes the final decision and selects the solution of her choice. Of course, one does have to know some alternatives. Our conversation continues.

"Some children let other children choose what game to play or let others go first."

"Sometimes it's easier to find someone who is playing by herself and ask her to play."

"Some children start a game or take a ball or jump rope or other toy and start playing with it."

"Sometimes children decide they want to play by themselves."

"Sometimes it's helpful to learn a way to ask to play that works."

"Which one would you like to try?" OR "What would you like to do?"

"I want to jump rope with that group."

"Let's practice these words so you can say them firmly. 'I want to play. Shall I twirl the jump rope or get in line to jump.'" *A statement rather than question, this involves a forced choice.*

When this child has practiced and feels ready, off she goes to try her new skill. Unfortunately, even a terrific line carries no guarantees. A group of children who has kept a child out is not very likely to include her just because she communicates more effectively. The leader may still say, "No, you can't play. Don't do either. Get away from here." So I increase the probability of success by walking behind the child; I will be close enough to hear and be noticed, far enough away to be unobtrusive. Have your ever noticed how children talk and behave differently when an adult is watching? (Eddie Haskell, where are you?) When the first child suggests that she wants to play, the child in command will look at her and start to say, "No!" but will then notice the adult present and immediately change to, "Well, go to the end of the line." We have a problem solved *by the child's actions.* Yes, I contributed, which is fine. We all like a little boost when we need it. Most importantly, the adult is neither the rescuer nor the one who selects the solution. We have effectively shared expertise and experience while still allowing the child the major role in solving her problem. We have reduced the risk of sabotage because the child owns the solution. We have taught a lesson in solving problems, we have helped a child increase her life skills, and we have sent excellent life messages. In *Celebrate Yourself*, Dorothy Briggs stated that past teaching can limit your options; her point is well taken. When children believe that they are <u>not</u> capable or that they regularly require rescue, their options become limited. However, the converse is also true, "past teaching can expand your options." When a child learns that she is capable and that she can solve problems with and without help, many options become available.

Life Lessons

The key to emotional health is in taking *some* action not the right action.

Not taking responsibility for directing our lives is as much a choice as taking this responsibility; both are decisions.

Life Messages

I can think and do for myself; I am capable. I can solve problems.

There is no problem so great I cannot handle it; I may need some help, but I know how to seek that, too.

It is of utmost importance that we teach all of our children that they have within themselves the capacity to solve problems. They may need help occasionally, but support and ideas are radically different from rescue. When they have a problem, all they need (for emotional health) is a plan of action they can and will take. No one needs to get overly excited or upset. It is not beneficial to seek fault or blame, rather it is important to look for helpful alternatives or solutions. They do not need ever to allow themselves to travel down the Victim Path.

No more self-made victims! No more helplessness!

Focus on what is right

Focus on what is right with them, not what is wrong.

Our roles as parents or teachers inherently include noticing what is wrong so that we can teach children how to change to what is correct, appropriate, or right. Children have so very much to learn; it is inevitable that they will come up with many wrongs. Too often and too quickly we pass over all that is right and point out the single thing that is wrong. A child arrives proud and smiling for breakfast on time, with shoes, matching socks, pants, and shirt. And we say, "Your shirt is on backwards." Goodbye smile and pride. This is classic discouragement. Almost all of us have heard our children complain, "You never see what's right, you just talk about what's wrong." They bring us a report card with A's in every subject but English. Too often, we ask, "Why did you get a C in English?" The alternative is to make sure we also address what has gone right along with what has gone wrong. The alternatives might sound like the following:

"You have your shoes and socks on; you even put your pants and shirt on, and you made it to the table before 7:15. You may want to turn your shirt around so that the tag is in the back and the neck doesn't ride so high." *Action started to remedy problem.*

As you back out of the garage, reply to the child who wails that he forgot his tennis shoes, "No, it seems you remembered them."

To the young child who has spilled paint: "You washed all the red paint off the table; now all you need is a fresh paper towel to dry the table."

"Look at all those A's. You must have worked hard and turned in your homework on time and studied for your tests." *Pride and smile.* "What do you think happened in English?" *Pride and smile still intact. Thoughtfulness and problem-solving begun.*

Self-pride and feeling good about accomplishments are developed and allowed to remain.

Life Lesson

One can view the glass as half empty or half full.

Show Value for Improvement or Effort

Celebrate small steps.

> People seldom see the halting and painful steps by which
> the most insignificant success is achieved. - Anne Sullivan,
> *The Story of My Life*, by Helen Keller

There is no reason to wait for perfection; it may be a long time arriving, if it comes at all. Too often we wait for completion, excellence, or perfection before we acknowledge success. Success comes in steps, any of which can be recognized and noticed. Improvement also generally comes in increments rather than all at once. There is no reason to wait for the final product or final achievement. We sacrifice no affirmation, the final success can be recognized as well.

"You've already pruned three trees. Pruning takes time and effort. Just two more to go."

"When you're ready, you'll swim all the way across the pool. Let's try it to the second lane again."

"We've worked hard. Let's take a break before we finish. How does a glass of ice water sound?"

"Learning to tie shoes is hard. You seem to have the first part of the knot."

"You've been working on that book report for twenty minutes now."

Life Lesson

Success is a journey, not a destination.

Encourage Each Child to Contribute

Allow and encourage each child to contribute to the family or class with ideas and action; help them strengthen their membership in the family, classroom, or group.

Contributing to a group provides two significant benefits. Contributing, whether with ideas (at home - where to go for a vacation, who does which chores, menu ideas; and at school - rules, special projects, field trip locations, agenda, academic ideas) or actions (at home - cleaning, cooking, laundry, errands, baby-sitting; and at school - cleaning up, moving chairs and tables, classroom tasks and responsibilities) increases self-esteem. Helping makes us feel better.

The second benefit is a strengthening of the bond with the group we assist and serve. We develop a sense of membership, of being not simply a part of a group, but an integral part. It is clear that more and more children and adolescents feel disconnected from and disenfranchised within their own homes and schools. They *belong* nowhere. A sense of belonging or of fitting in somewhere is vital to young children and becomes an even larger issue for adolescents. Society's failure to help children feel this has left many children lost and vulnerable. There is an organization which is snatching up these children and doing a superb job of making them feel and be a part of the group. What is this organization? Gangs.

Gangs are an expanding threat to our children and to our nation. Gangs are excellent at recruiting and keeping members. National statistics are vague because it is difficult to determine accurate numbers concerning gang membership and crime. But if we look at a typical medium sized city and county, Fort Worth in Tarrant County, Texas, the statistics are chilling. According to the Texas Attorney General Gang report, there were 119 active gangs in Fort Worth and 1,657 identified gang members. The next year, the Texas Association for the Education of Young Children reported 215 gangs.

Sometimes when I am speaking to a group about creating a sense of belonging and membership and commitment, I feel as though I ought to have a gang leader helping me; they are frighteningly successful. Keep in mind that gang members routinely commit crimes *for the gang*; they are willing not just to wear "uniforms" and behave in a prescribed fashion, but also to steal, assault, and murder. Some children are unwilling to do dishes for the family, but will kill for their gang. Unfortunately, we have much to learn from gangs. And we are paying a huge price financially, socially, and often individually, in the meantime.

Consider also that, according to the Children's Defense Fund, nationwide 2,255 teenagers drops out of high school each day. The Department of Labor has estimated that by 1994 three out of four jobs will require not only a high school diploma, but training beyond the high school level. In Texas, each dropout is estimated to cost the state $203,488, and 93% of Texas prison inmates never completed high school.[13] Further it costs Texas taxpayers nearly $14,000 each year to incarcerate an inmate.[14] Not belonging at school costs all of us. Not just in taxes, but with fear of violence.

Where will our children find a place to belong, a place where they can become valuable and contributing members? It hurts not to belong; even a bad group is better than no group. Are our children made to feel they are genuinely an integral part of our families, our classrooms, our schools? Will business welcome them? Or will the gangs be the only group welcoming them? That choice is ours. We have them first.

Life Lessons

Belonging somewhere is important to emotional well-being.

Contributing helps one bond to the group. Contributing is an essential part of membership.

Contributing feels good and builds self-esteem.

Focus on Capabilities

Help each child see himself as capable and essential.

They are able because they think they are able. - Virgil

Keep in mind that we, the important adults in a given child's life, are the mirrors from which she will determine largely who she is. Are we careful to reflect capable and essential, as well as valuable and likeable, or do we too often reflect to a child a sense of incompetence, uselessness, helplessness, dispensability? We must monitor both our words and our actions. We are sometimes unhelpful:

"Here, let me tie that for you."
"I'll do it, never mind; it's not worth arguing with you."
"All you ever do is watch TV; nobody ever helps."
"No, I'd rather do the laundry myself. It has to be done right." "Did you remember to thank Mrs. Watson?"
"Did you play nicely?"

Do you redo a job you have given a child to complete?
Are your children little princes or contributors?
Do your children offer to help you with tasks?

Do your children believe that they can do a job well by their own
   standards and by yours?
Do your children have increasing responsibilities and increasing freedom?

Do you pack your child's bag for overnight and small trips?
Do you pack your teen's bag for a week's vacation?
Can your children cook?
Can you send your children off to play or to school or to visit friends with
   a simple, "Goodbye, have a good time," and leave out all the extra
   baggage, "Be good, don't forget to say thank you, wear your jacket..."

By the time they are ready to leave home, will they have learned enough
household management skills, money management skills, self-discipline skills
- *life management skills* - to not just survive but to thrive on their own?

   Your behavior will match your picture of yourself. - Alexander
   Dumas

The self-fulfilling prophecy has been recognized for generations. It is
obvious that if we tell a child by our words or actions, "You are ___fill in
description__" often enough, he will become more and more _same description_.
What we see and project to him is what he begins to resemble. In this way
past teaching not only can but does limit options. We must be very careful
about what color of glasses we put on to look through, for rosy and golden
glasses see the potential good and grace in a child, and dark and gray
glasses see only the potential problems and misery.

We can choose to deal with any time frame or verb tense - past, present,
or future. Here are some examples of Historian (past), Reporter (present),
and Prophet (future).

To the child struggling to learn to swim:
Historian: "I remember a child who was afraid to get his face wet."
Reporter: "I see a child who can swim all the way to the second lane."
Prophet: "When you're ready, you'll be able to swim to the other side by
                yourself." (I love this phrasing; did you ever meet a child
                who did anything before he was ready?)

♜ To the young child who cannot get the straps on her overalls buttoned:

Historian: "I remember a girl who couldn't pull up her own slacks."

Reporter: "You can pull on slacks and shirts, and you know how to put on your shoes."

Prophet: "When you're ready, you'll be able to handle overalls all by yourself."

🍎 To the student who is having difficulty with multiplication:

Historian: "In Kindergarten, you didn't know any addition facts; adding was hard then."

Reporter: "You seem to understand the process; it's just remembering all the different multiplication facts that's difficult right now."

Prophet: "Once you've mastered the multiplication facts, you'll have it!"

Life Lesson

Accomplishments frequently take time and effort.

Law of the Farm: Most things must be learned and accomplished by taking the correct steps in the correct order, in their own time. If you only water when you plant the seeds, nothing will come to fruition.

Children learn patience and the concept, ONE STEP AT A TIME.

Life Message

I have succeeded before, I will succeed again. I *am* capable.

Trait: Confidence

The trait that accompanies self-esteem built in this area of Accomplishment is Confidence. Children who have tried at anything and have been effective, productive, or triumphant begin to build confidence, a firm belief that they have tried and succeeded before and will again. We know that success succeeds and that getting things right, mastering something, being productive, *accomplishing anything, large or small,* feels good and builds our self-confidence and our self-esteem.

Please keep in mind, success or accomplishments are much like baseball. They are meant to be fun, not life-threatening.

14:
Mistakes

LIFE MESSAGE: There is No Problem So Great I Cannot Handle It - I Can Get
It Right - I *am* Capable
TRAIT: Courage

Misfortune comes to all men. - Chinese proverb

This category of self-esteem has so much potential, and yet it is the area where we regularly diminish self-esteem rather than enhance it. We both waste and corrupt opportunities to build self-esteem. As pointed out previously, this area offers the quickest and most dramatic boost in self-esteem. The two most important factors determining whether we boost or shatter self-esteem are our true attitude toward mistakes and our skill with criticism - are we hurtful or helpful, encouraging or discouraging. First, let us address our attitude toward mistakes.

Opportunities for Learning

Is it alright for your children or students to make mistakes? How many times? Do you handle the third episode with the same grace as the first? Do you handle behavioral mistakes - mis(taken)behavior with the same attitude as academic or social mistakes? Is it acceptable for you to make a mistake? Are you sure? Perhaps it would be helpful to check your genuine attitude.

The last time you could not locate your car keys, what did you say to yourself? When I present this concept in a live seminar, I always ask if we should do a 'sharing time' with the messages we send to ourselves. No group ever wants to do this. I rarely can find a participant who said anything remotely positive to himself. If this is true for you, I respectfully suggest that your integrity on this issue may be out of kilter. What we say we believe or want to believe and what we practice are at odds. What our heads believe differs from what our hearts believe. Our attitude is not so clean as we want and as we need it to be.

Do we believe and practice that mistakes are the last step or the first step of a process? When a mistake is the last step of a process, we end up with a failed person. This is not beneficial to self-esteem. When, alternatively, we view a mistake as the first step of a process, a problem-solving or learning process, we end up with a failed situation - *which can be changed*. No problem to self-esteem.

There was a time in my life when I had a toddler, just toilet trained, and an infant, breast fed. We lived in Canada, and it was still quite cold outside, still snowsuit weather. If you have never stuffed a toddler into a snow suit, you have not experienced parenthood in its fullness. We had just driven home, so I know I had just had my keys in my possession. As we got to the door of our house, I had a screaming, hungry baby and a toddler in his snow suit doing the newly-trained-I-really-have-to-go-peepee-now dance. I could hear my keys in my purse, but I could not find them. It was on this day that I began to truly change my attitude toward mistakes. For in this turmoil, after berating myself and doggedly trying to keep from crying, I became determined to never let my keys get the better of me again. I was never going to get caught like this again. *This situation* was stupid, but *I* was not. I could beat it. The next outing, I found a purse with a key ring that snapped into the top of the purse; I bought it. I still have it (and several like it), and I still use the snap. And my keys do not beat me anymore. I handled it. This is clearly a small victory over an inanimate foe; it still feels wonderful.

Mistakes are opportunities for learning; they tell us clearly what we need to learn or teach.

To lose is to learn. - unknown

Without this heart-felt belief about mistakes, we are destined to model and reveal our less helpful attitude that mistakes tell us how stupid we are, that mistakes are bad, and that smart or good or capable people should not and do not make them. Is it any wonder then that many children will lie, cheat, hide, or run away from their mistakes? Most vulnerable are those children whose self-esteem is tied up in Accomplishment. As noted previously, "whenever personal worth is dependent upon performance, personal value is subject to cancellation with every misstep."

Almost anything is better than feeling you have no value, including lying to yourself and others or cheating or disclaiming any ownership and responsibility for the mistake. At all costs, the true outcome - you are not the best or you did not succeed - must be avoided. It is easy to see how hurtful and scary genuinely owning a mistake can be for children in this situation; this is why self-esteem must first come from Existence and why the correct attitude toward mistakes is impossible without self-esteem firmly established in this primary area. Everyone makes mistakes; what we need to do is own them and then learn from them.

Parents have disparate attitudes toward mistakes, and consequently have different ways of coaching children. Some styles are more helpful than others. Here are examples of two very dissimilar parents. This time we play basketball.

Basketball is a complex game of strategy and skill. When played by young children, it is a most amazing game; it does not much resemble college or even high school basketball. The year my younger son, Tim, was eleven his team happened to be quite good. They had several strong players. They had managed to easily beat every team they played - until the last game. That last game they came up against a team who was better. For the first time that season, they found themselves behind.

On Tim's team there happened to be a boy, we will call him Bob, who was under tremendous pressure by his parents to do well, to quite literally be the star - in everything, not just sports. Bob was good at being the star. He handled the ball more than anyone else; he shot and scored more than anyone else. He would finally pass the ball when he found himself trapped, but then would immediately call to have it passed back. It is easy to guess that Bob was not much of a team player. He could not afford to pass the ball to an open man; they might score, or worse still, outscore Bob. He was neither a play maker nor a team leader; he was too absorbed in himself. He had to be the star. Anything less was unacceptable to his father. Throughout every game, Bob's father exhorted him to shoot, get the ball, score: "Come on, Bob, shoot! It's up to *you* to score! *You* have to win this game!" During the course of the season, Bob's father had managed to alienate all of the other parents; there were, after all, other children on the team and on the court.

During that last game, as the other team pulled farther and farther ahead, Bob's father became increasingly insistent and loud. He was unrelenting in his yelling to Bob. "Bob, *you're* behind. *You* have to shoot! Shoot, Bob, shoot! Get the ball, Bob!" Mr. Bob was directing Bob virtually every moment. The change in Bob as the game progressed was dramatic. At the beginning of the game, Bob would only shoot when he had a clear, close shot, and only from inside the foul line. Soon, in desperation, he was shooting from center court. Bob was a small eleven year old. He did not have the proverbial snowball's chance to hit the backboard from there, let alone score. Still Bob's father exhorted him. It was inconceivable and intolerable that Bob could *let* this team lose. Late in the fourth quarter, Bob came down the court with the ball, shot it wildly, and missed the backboard. His father hollered, "Bob, *you* can't afford to miss like that!" Bob froze. Then he turned to his father, and in a clear voice said, "F--k off, Dad!" Despite the profanity and disrespect, many of us in the stands silently cheered his remark. Bob's father's coaching style clearly hindered Bob's performance. It also sabotaged self-esteem, violated their bond, and was unhealthy. I am concerned whenever a parent needs to build his own self-esteem through the successes of his child. The team lost the game; Bob and his father lost something greater.

The next season my son returned to the basketball court with a differently configured, intramural team - new teammates and new coach, his own father. For those of you who have not witnessed youth intramural basketball, it is important to understand that the early games of the season are frequently enlivened by moments of Bozo basketball. Anything can happen. Plays are disorganized, and skills are not honed yet. Early in the first game of the season, Tim managed to steal the ball while one of his teammates still remained back in their own end of the court. Having this open man near his own basket, Tim seized the opportunity and threw the ball to him as hard as he could. Unfortunately, Tim had overlooked the fact that he had grown two inches and gained ten pounds since the previous basketball season. Fortunately, the ball sailed harmlessly past his teammate and smashed into the wall at the opposite end of the court. Big mistake, a missed opportunity for an undefended, easy lay-up, quick two points. Tim immediately looked over to his dad-coach. It is not unusual at times like this to see coaches frown and shake their heads, pull the player, or ask why he did that - as if the player knew or meant to do it. Tim's dad chose another path. He smiled and laughed and shook his head to acknowledge Bozo ball. It had been funny to see the look of surprise on Tim's face when he realized he had actually thrown the basketball that far. Freed from guilt and discouragement, Tim laughed too, and raised his hands palms upward to acknowledge that he had had no idea he could throw like that either. The rest of his game was not flawless; it was still that first game. But he played better and better, and his value and confidence were still intact. One simply needs to learn from one's mistakes. And sometimes, mistakes are pretty harmless and awfully funny. It is a gift to be able to laugh at yourself. I cannot remember whether they won that game; I do know that Tim and his dad won.

Jeff Salzman, co-founder of CareerTrack®, in his audio tape program, How to Get Results With People™ describes CareerTrack's handling of mistakes. Whenever an employee makes a mistake, he fills out a mistake form. The form includes three sections.

Mistake I will NEVER make again:
Steps I took to minimize this mistake's consequences or effect:
Steps I have taken to prevent this mistake from ever occurring again:

Mistake I will never make again.   This speaks to ownership of the mistake. When someone denies or avoids ownership by lying or covering up the mistake, responsibility is bypassed, learning from the mistake is much less likely to occur, and the mistake's consequences may grow. (Spilled milk sours, the bathtub continues to overflow, a student gets further and further behind.)

Our house, like many others in neighborhoods with children, has had a window broken, not by the proverbial baseball but by a golf ball. The actual breaking of the window did not anger me; I expected that sooner or later this would happen.   What did irritate me was the fact that no one claimed ownership and told us about it. We had to discover it ourselves. It happened in the dining room, a room we are not in every day. Had it rained before we discovered it, drapes, carpet, and windowsill would have been damaged. It is not the mistake that I begrudge; it is the failure to own it.

Steps I have taken to minimize the effects or consequences of this mistake. This looks after damage control. Isn't that what is most important after the mistake has occurred? If you have spilled the milk, all I really expect is that you clean it up so that I do not have to, so that it does not smell, and so that I do not sit down on a sticky, dirty chair. When you break something, all I expect is that you fix or replace it. This is Damage Control.

As adults in the work world, we recognize mistakes will happen. Owners, employers, managers, administrators seek minimized effects.

Steps I have taken to prevent this mistake from occurring again. This last declaration points out that when we learn from a mistake, we are more able to avoid it in the future. It is someone's repeated mistakes that make us crazy. It is at the third or fourth time a child spills milk in one meal when we lose our calm and our grace.

As your parent or teacher or even as your co-worker, I want to be assured that I do not have to worry about this mistake again; I need to know that you have learned from this mistake, that it was not in vain.

Interestingly, Mr. Salzman reports that at CareerTrack, a very fast-growing, leading edge company, each staff member fills out a form for every mistake and then brings these forms to his annual review. At CareerTrack, if you have *too few* Mistake forms, you are asked to leave and seek employment with a more conservative company because *clearly you have not taken enough risks, demonstrated enough courage, and learned enough* to work with a fast-paced, thriving company. This is a novel concept.

This form is a wonderful addition to detention where students generally waste time or do homework. Filling out this Mistake form pertaining to the deed which brought a student to detention ensures she knows exactly why she is here, promotes ownership and responsibility for the deed, fosters ideas for minimizing effects, teaches damage control as an important aspect of making mistakes, and clears the path to preventing this deed's repeated occurrence. In short, it promotes learning from mistakes.

Life Lessons

Everyone makes mistakes.

Mistakes create opportunities for learning.

Mistakes require damage control and amends.

In the end, when I solve my problem, remedy or make amends for my mistake, or learn something the hard way, my self-esteem grows.

Separate the Deed from the Doer?
Or Do We Own Our Actions?

With self-esteem intact in all three areas, we no longer have to be afraid of mistakes and the damage they could do to our sense of self-worth. It was this fear coupled with the knowledge that telling a child we do not like him is detrimental to the child and to our bond or relationship, that led us to the "Separate the Deed from the Doer" concept. For years, we have been taught never to tell a child we do not like him; rather, we are to tell him that we do not like what he has done. This constitutes separating the deed from the doer. It is past time to shatter this concept; it is untruthful, harmful, and dangerous. Again, like so many dealing with people and communication skills, we started with a concept which helped us take a more helpful direction; yet like technological inventions, we need to make improvements. Early models always seem to have 'bugs' in them. Two major pitfalls are inherent in the concept "I like you, but I don't like your behavior."

First, it simply is not true. In the real world, we do not separate deed and doer. In live sessions, I ask participants the following series of questions to prove this point.

When you meet someone, how do you determine if you like that person? How do you decide whether or not you might be friends? The universal answer I receive is by what they do, by their actions. Could we not call this their behavior? We decide whom we like by whether or not we like their behavior. In truth, we do not separate deed and doer. Let us go one step farther. Do you like murderers? No? Then let us talk about serial killers, the worst of the murderers. Even serial killers spend less than one per cent of their lives killing people. The rest of the time, many of them are model citizens with excellent behavior; this is what makes them so very difficult to catch. So, are you willing to invite these serial killers to dinner at your house for one behavior which occupies less than one per cent of their time? No, absolutely not. I rest my case. We do not separate deed and doer.

Secondly, it is harmful to separate deed from doer because this undermines discipline. Fundamental to discipline is this concept, *You are responsible for what you choose to do and for what happens to you and others as a result of your decisions and actions.* Owning your behavior, owning all of your behavior is the foundation of discipline that leads to self-discipline and to responsibility. We corrupt our own discipline with this "separate deed and doer." We have also sent two mixed messages to our youth. First, with discipline, we tell them they must own their behavior. With "I like you, but not your behavior" we tell them you are separate from your behavior, you do not have to own it after all. Then consider what we have done with praise. For years, we have told children that we like this behavior or that behavior and hoped they would own it and feel better about themselves because they had done something right or good. Thus, we have told them that when your behavior is acceptable, you own it. When it is unacceptable, you do not. No wonder children are confused.

Certainly, earlier pathfinders were partly right. It is harmful to children to tell them we do not like them. The bind came into play because we did not know how to tell a child that something he has done or failed at (behavior, academics, mistake) is not good enough. We did not know how to criticize without being discouraging and hurtful, rather than encouraging and helpful. Yet children need to be told, and as parents or teachers, telling them is a major component of our job description. We are all aware that we need to be encouraging not discouraging and that the times we cause the most discouragement are when the child has made a mistake. The question, then, is how can we get ourselves out of this bind? How can we tell a child that he is off the mark and still encourage rather than discourage? The answer is DESCRIPTIVE CRITICISM.

Life Lesson

I own *everything* I do. My behavior tells me and others *who I am.*

Descriptive Criticism
Criticism that encourages rather than discourages.

> I have yet to find the man - however exalted his station -
> who did not do better work and put forth greater effort under
> a spirit of approval than under a spirit of criticism. - Charles
> Schwab

Mr. Schwab was absolutely correct. Classic criticism hurts and discourages. It passes judgment or evaluates. It leaves the recipient feeling less capable and disheartened, and she is less likely to learn from the mistake and repair it. Criticism that encourages leaves the recipient feeling intact, capable, and more able to remedy and learn.

Helpful criticism is future oriented and empowering. It focuses not on what is wrong, but on what changes need to be made. It teaches by describing actions needed; it does not evaluate or attack character.

Two jobs which seem to require criticizing children are teacher and coach. Parents also criticize. In order to teach children life lessons, life skills, academics, or athletics, we must, at times, point out to them mistakes, failures, or deficiencies. Too often the end result is discouragement rather than encouragement. Coaches can be either a nightmare or a dream come true. They are the difference between a long season and a short season; sometimes they are the difference between a child loving or abandoning a sport.

When we moved to Texas, my elder son re-entered baseball after one season of Tee-Ball (where the batters hit a ball off a large tee) and one season entirely missed due to a broken arm. Needless to say, his batting skills were minimal. I arrived at the end of one practice and watched as one of his two coaches struggled to help him learn to hit the ball. The coach would throw the ball; my son would swing and miss. The coach watched and then told him, "Don't bail out." Coach pitches, Kris swings and misses. "Swing, son, don't bail out," reminded the coach. As I watched, each became increasingly frustrated. Then I could almost see the light come on in the coach's head. A smile came across his face. This time before he pitched the ball, he said, "Kris, when I throw the ball, I want you to take your front foot, your right foot (Kris is left-handed) and step forward - move it towards me when you swing." Kris steps forward with his right foot and miraculously hits the ball. What worked? Telling him what *to do* rather than telling him what *not to do*. His other coach worked with him on bunting as well; bunting forces a batter to watch the ball. Did he become a fantastic hitter overnight? No, but he began his journey to better hitting which two years later found him as the lead off batter and bunter par excellence. Not bad coaching!

At times, it is helpful to include what not to do; generally only when what not to do is preventing the successful completion of what to do. However, telling what not to do is more often not necessary, and *telling what not to do by itself is never enough*. Far more helpful is describing what needs to be changed or done to correct the mistake, improve the deficit, or remedy the oversight.

By the nature of our work with children, we must criticize. It is our job to point out when they are off the mark and need to do better. There is a synonym or alternative word for criticize - one with which we will all be comfortable. For none of us is truly comfortable with criticism; it has become a word with a very negative connotation. I am frequently asked how to make bad news sound good. Each of us has been in a situation where we have been discouraged by criticism. So, too, have we been in a situation where seemingly magically, someone has helped us see our mistake or misstep and improve. We ended up encouraged and feeling better about ourselves. How was this done? It is helpful to compare classic criticism with descriptive criticism. In the process, we will discover the synonym which can forever and always replace the term criticize. You will never need to criticize again; still you will be able to communicate to a child or adult, "This is not good enough; you can get it right." First classic, common, discouraging criticism.

Early in first grade, my son arrived home from school, threw a paper down on the kitchen table, and pronounced, "My teacher says I can't write." If we pause right here, how would you guess he will write tomorrow? Worse or not at all. He is definitely discouraged. I picked up his paper and immediately saw two things. First, across the top of his paper were written the words, "Very poor handwriting." This is classic criticism which evaluates performance negatively. Second, I noticed that this was truly some of the worst printing I had ever seen. Indeed, the teacher's point was accurate; my son needed to do better. I looked at my son and remarked, "I know what teachers call good writing."

My son looked at me and said, "I'm hungry." Never try to work with a child who is tired or hungry. He snacked; he played outside. Later he returned and warily asked, "So, what do teachers think is good writing?"

Now it is time for helpful, encouraging, descriptive criticism. He has opened himself up to me, and he is vulnerable. He can be quickly discouraged; he has already been burned once on this issue. Still, he has given to me a wonderful opportunity to help him *get it right*. "Well," I answer, "they like the letters to rest on the lines, like this one and this one."

"I can do that," he responded as he printed several letters on the blank lines at the bottom of the sheet of paper. "What else do they want?"

"They like to have small, even spaces between the letters in a word, about like the spaces between those two," I said as I pointed to two good examples.

"Anyone can do that," he said more confidently as he again showed me he could. "What else do they want?" he repeated.

"They like to have bigger spaces between the words so they can tell which letters go with which words."

Again, as he showed me the desired improvement, "That's easy; I can do that! See my teacher doesn't know anything; I can too write."

Pause here and forecast how he will write the next day in his class. I bet he will show her just what he can do! Encouraged? Yes. Who wins? He does - he can now write more legibly. His teacher does - she will have what she was after - improved writing from him. I do - I helped facilitate this outcome.

Now, the synonym for criticize. What did I do that so magically and quickly encouraged? Pause for a moment; think about this. Rarely do entire groups come up with the answer. What I did and what you would easily have recognized, if I had not placed this story in the realm of criticism and merely described my telling him about letter placement and spacing, is called *TEACHING*. Albeit, more accurately, it was re-teaching; I am quite certain that his first grade teacher had mentioned placing letters on the lines before. Imagine, a child, a bright child, who did not tune into or act upon his first teaching! Know any adults who require re-teaching? Have you ever required a second lesson? A third lesson? We need never criticize again. No more evaluation; no more blame; only teaching is needed.

Teaching or if you prefer *Descriptive Criticism* simply describes what needs to be done for improvement or change. When mistakes are made or improvement is needed, *teaching* is the tool of choice. *Teaching* nets results, encouragement, and high self-esteem. Classic criticism is never needed.

When we do not seem to be able to get through to another and we are frustrated by continued, repeated mistakes, deficiency, or lack of improvement, it is time for us to re-evaluate. Is there a better way or method to teach this lesson to this particular child? Is this child developmentally ready for the required task or skills, or should we wait? What mistake are we making? What is getting in the way of this child's learning?

As adults, this format continues to be helpful and productive. Most of us have been evaluated at a job. Sometimes we leave the evaluation with only numbers (evaluation) and discouragement. But every once in awhile, a gifted evaluator appears. The outcome of this session can be very different - helpful, encouraging, and productive.

One group subjected to periodic evaluations is teachers. Some evaluators leave us with a number-ranked evaluation and comments which are best described as classic criticism. "Well, Mrs. Smith, you smile quite a bit, but too often your students are not paying attention so I had to lower your mark in this area. Your lessons seem to be adequate; you just don't seem to be able to pull them back to you when their attention wanders. They are not learning what you are teaching."

How does one feel after such an encounter? Terrible, embarrassed, angry, saddened, discouraged? Thoughts may include, "I thought I was *meant* to be a teacher, but maybe I'm in over my head. Maybe I should leave education, maybe I'm just not cut out to be a teacher." Classic discouragement contributes directly to burnout, a problem in many fields, including education. This was not the evaluator's goal or purpose, but it was the net result.

What if, on the other hand, the evaluator used the evaluation form and time to teach? What if only master teachers could be evaluators? What if the comments sounded like this: "Mrs. Smith, thank you for including me in your classroom. I have included strong ratings on many items which I will let you peruse at your leisure, I will not spend our valuable time on those items now. My job is to help you strengthen weaker areas. One of the things I noticed that you struggled with was maintaining individual student's attention at times. It happens in every class at one time or another. Students, especially some types of students, fade in and out despite interesting lessons, and I found your lessons well-paced, engaging, and thought-provoking. Would it be helpful to discuss some of the strategies other teachers have used to bring back individual fading students?" After a brief discussion of tips such as moving around the room while teaching, standing beside students, including students in discussion, this teacher is able to leave the evaluation with these thoughts: "I did a number of things well, but I need to get better at noticing students when they are not paying attention. I *can* do that. And I *can* help them. I *can* walk around the room more during discussions and lectures. *I can do better. I can do this. I can handle this!* I'm not the perfect teacher yet, but I'm on my way." Encouraged? Yes. Burned out? No, fired up.

Teaching is the remedy to mistakes and the alternative to criticism. Teaching is the key to encouragement.

We are all aware of how important it is to be encouraging rather than discouraging. Now you know how to accomplish this.

Life Lesson

Mistakes signal the need for teaching, not criticizing. Teaching can entirely replace criticism.

Life Message

I can get it right. I can solve my problems. I can learn.

Immunize Against Discouragement

Included here is a note on the damage done by others; for classic criticism is going to continue to exist. Others will criticize our children; others will belittle them; others will cause discouragement. We must include two important lessons for our children to strengthen their resistance and immunity to these negative influences. Eleanor Roosevelt stated the first lesson concisely and beautifully:

"No one can make you feel inferior without your permission."

Or as phrased by a child, "It is not what they think, it's what I know."[15] We are the ultimate judges of who we are and how much value we have. We determine this within ourselves. And we must not give this capacity and power away. We must help children to recognize that what they believe and know about themselves is more significant and generally more accurate than what others believe. We can help them become less vulnerable to criticism and belittling by others. I frequently find myself in a situation where a child comes to me saying someone has called her a name; I recognize this as an opportunity to teach this concept. The conversation invariably follows these lines:

"Jimmy called me stupid."
"Well, do you think you're stupid?"
Thoughtful pause. "No, I know lots of things."
"So, then, you believe Jimmy is mistaken?"
Short pause again. "Yes, I'm pretty smart."
"There you are! It's not what he thinks; it's what you know!"
"Yes, it's what *I* know!" Accompanied by a smile.

The heart of the second lesson is simply conceding the passage of time. That was then; this is now.

Have you ever considered the amount of freedom granted by this statement? Being able to wipe the slate clean and start over is important in any relationship and for all of us; it is particularly important for children who develop and change daily. The younger the child, the more vast is the difference between any *then* and *now*; they learn so rapidly, they sleep and forget, they simply forget, and they rarely hold grudges. For relationships to be healthy and to thrive, *forgive and forget* must be included and repeated. Without these, all of the ever present minor digressions and irritations begin to add up and accumulate. *That was then, this is now* fortifies healthy relationships.

There are a few experiences which may be forgiven but the lessons learned need never to be forgotten. The holocaust is one. Sexual abuse is another. The other side of the coin is that we need to beware of holding onto mistakes (especially within families and close friendships) and virtually keeping a tally of them. All families, all relationships have positive and negative experiences involved. Again, we can choose which type to focus on and remember.

Life Lessons

Our evaluation of ourselves is the most important.

That was then; this is now. We can choose to dwell on the past or we can choose to move forward from here. Courage is the ability to try and fail and to try again.

Take Time to Teach

Use mistakes and misbehavior as the opportunities for teaching that they are. But this means *taking time to teach.* It generally takes longer to teach a child than to ignore, punish, or manipulate around inappropriate behavior. It also takes longer and requires less effort and thought in the short term to teach rather than to do something right or remedy a mistake yourself. The latter also fall into the "spend, spend, spend" category - saving time only when viewed in the immediate short term, but devouring substantially more time in the long run. Teaching requires an *investment* of time now, yet over the long term, teaching consumes considerably less time. Again, the import of seeing and playing to the long term cannot be emphasized enough.

Although patience and skill are indispensable components of teaching, I believe that in these fast-paced, harried, hurried times, that *time* is the component which most frequently impedes or prevents teaching. Dolores Curran, tells about an incisive article found in the October, 1979 *Harper's* and written by Louis T. Grant.[16] He entitled the article "Fast Folk" and dissects an earlier article published in *Woman's Day* which had praised the fast-paced lifestyle of one mother.

Listen to this woman's life. She rushes from home to work in the morning, eating yogurt in the car for breakfast; has lunch at the spa where she works out; leaves child care to her husband, who also has a managerial position forty miles the other side of home; pilots a small plane in her leisure time for pleasure; teaches on the side a class at a local women's college; leaves the kids with Grandma; leaves the kids with sitters; leaves the kids...."

Mr. Grant labeled these people 'fast folk'; know anyone who falls into this category? He likened this life style to keeping up with the gerbils. Hits home does it not? There is no time for other members of the family, for intimacy, for building communication, for teaching important Life Lessons. These, the author says, are for slowpokes. And, by the way, he also points out that children are slowpokes - bless their hearts. In the 1990's we are still prone to glorify this type of lifestyle. We still struggle with tangible signs of productivity, of Accomplishment, of value. When did 'producing' a healthy family, with emotionally healthy, happy, stable children stop being important, stop being a major accomplishment? Are we so hooked into immediate gratification that we must see tangible proof of production daily? That *only* concrete proof counts? That without proof we have no value? We have lost our grounding, our focus, and our center. Perhaps I am tired of hearing so many people espouse family values as they eschew their own family. I confess it is exceedingly easy to get lost in ourselves, our jobs, and our chores and to lose not just our balance but our own sense of values, our own principles. I continue to catch myself behaving at odds with my principles (with my integrity yet again disintegrating); I have told my own children to get a grip, stop quarreling, and leave me alone so that I can finish this book. (I know, nice touch!) But I also admit to putting the book on hold while I *chose* to take time to be with my family. I am not suggesting that we quit jobs, take neither leisure nor alone time, nor forget about household chores. I am suggesting that too many of us have lost our control over our lives, and we have become time-stressed beyond belief and beyond health.

If you do not make time to teach your child principles, such as responsibility for actions and respectful communication, and practices, such as how to fold clothes and a more efficient way to avoid spills, who will? And what will be the cost of these lost lessons to our children and to all of us?

As teachers, are we lost in the time-stress of teaching academics so that our students do well on standardized tests? Do we take time to teach individuals rather than teach material, subjects, or a class?

Life Lessons

Teaching (or learning) is an extremely worthwhile investment of time.

One of our most important gifts and legacies to our children is the time we spend with them.

I believe that the second most common component which impedes teaching is exasperation caused by stress from outside, unrelated sources, and lack of understanding or knowledge about children in general. All of these lead to unrealistic expectations. Too many people have not taken the time to learn at least a little about *children,* about their stages of development, about normal expectations. This information truly makes life and decision making much easier. It is important to learn about children in general and your own individual children specifically.

Beware of Negative Expectations

Do you expect that your child will do a poor job cleaning up the kitchen? Or will nastily push her brother around? Do you expect a student to do a mediocre job writing his book report? To not pay attention? We must always strive to be aware of our own negative expectations and of sending the message, "You can't get it right; you won't do better." The self-fulfilling prophecy is ever-present. Both our language (especially with regard to the disrespectful BARRIERS TO COOPERATION) and our actions (usually unconscious but not unnoticed) tell children who we think they are. In turn, the children tend to take these messages to heart. Be careful what messages you send: they will be received. Negative expectations yield negative results.

Life Lessons

The self-fulfilling prophecy can work for us or against us. This choice is ours.

Trait: Courage

Help them back up on the horse.

Take risks: if you win, you will be happy; if you lose, you will
be wise. - unknown

The trait which accompanies self-esteem built in the Mistakes category
is courage. Remember the old story that advocates putting a child right back
on his horse after he has fallen. Otherwise, courage diminishes and fear
grows. Once again, courage is trying and failing and *trying again.* We must
all learn to reclimb the horse. We may need to ask for help, to learn new
skills, to seek an alternative approach, but we need to reface our mistake and
try again.

One of my favorite definitions of courage (from the French word *coeur*,
meaning heart) is that courage is the ability to try and to fail and to try again.
It is reported that it took Thomas Edison more than a thousand trials to
discover the successful format for the electric light bulb. This certainly
represents courage, a trait all researchers and inventors must have. If we are
going to find a cure for AIDS, continue to make gains against various cancers
and other life-threatening diseases, invent better artificial limbs,
communication devices, and ways to technologically improve our lives, know
that these will all, most assuredly, be found by persons with this type of
courage, with self-esteem built in all three areas, including Mistakes. When
it was pointed out to Mr. Edison that he had *failed* over a thousand times, it
is recounted that he replied that he had figured out over a thousand ways
that a light bulb will not work. What a marvelous attitude!

It is the trying again, not the ultimate success, that is important.

Life Message

I have courage.

Affirming Practice
- Parents

What will you say and do? Be specific.

PRESCHOOLERS
1. Joey spills his milk, again.
2. Melissa arrives home looking happy and excited.
3. Kris has reversed three of five *S's*.
4. Tim brings you a picture he has just finished and asks you, "Do you like it? Is it good?"
5. Haley informs you that Eric just took the beach ball from Robin.

SCHOOL AGE
6. Joey's clothes are stuffed in his drawer, again.
7. Melissa arrives home cheerful and pleasant.
8. Martha brings you her homework paper and asks you, "Is it good enough?"
9. Your first baseman just missed an easy catch at first, caught two fly balls, failed to make an important throw to home, laid a bunt down the third base line which barely went foul, and stole second and third.

TEENS
10. Joe's done a terrible job mowing the lawn, again.
11. Melissa arrives home cheerful and excited.
12. Martha brings you her history report and asks you, "Is this good enough?"
13. Your teen, left in charge of two younger sisters for three hours, let other children in to play (not allowed), kept the phone busy for thirty minutes, made and cleaned up lunch for all of them, and handled a minor cut.
14. Robin informs you that Eric just took the remote control and started watching his show.

Affirming Practice
- Early Childhood Educators
What will you say and do? Be specific.

1. Joey tears his picture with his eraser, again.

2. Melissa returns from playing outside looking happy and excited.

3. Kris has reversed three of five *S's*.

4. Tim brings you a picture he has just finished and asks you, "Do you like it? Is it good?"

5. Haley informs you that Eric just took the beach ball from Robin.

Affirming Practice
- Teachers

What will you say and do? Be specific.

ELEMENTARY SCHOOL

1. Joey tears his paper with his eraser, again.

2. Melissa arrives in class cheerful and excited.

3. Martha brings you her history paper and asks you, "Is this good enough?"

4. Robert's bibliography is not alphabetized, nor are the entries in any organized form.

5. Robin informs you that Eric just copied his paper.

MIDDLE AND HIGH SCHOOL

6. Joe's done a terrible job on his book report again.

7. Melissa arrives in class cheerful and excited.

8. Martha brings you her history report and asks you, "Is this good enough?"

9. Robert's project is poorly organized and does not follow the assigned format.

10. Robin informs you that Eric just cheated on his test.

15:
Self-Esteem Summary

What You See is What You Get

Years ago, comedian Flip Wilson portrayed a brash, sexy woman named Geraldine. One of Geraldine's favorite remarks, made to a man and made with swaying hips and shoulders was, "What you see is what you get." Geraldine's point differs from mine, but her words are right on target. If we see our children as problems, they will be. If we see our children as wonderful gifts with the potential for civilization, they will become so. Invariably, what we look for and perceive is what we uncover and find. This quick quote blends the concepts of self-fulfilling prophecy and focus on what is right with them. We select the color of lenses through which we peer. **Think *before* you see.**

> You never know when a moment and a few sincere words
> can have an impact on a life. - Zig Ziglar

Teachers have profoundly influenced children's lives. Many stories have been written about this. It is not the children with high self-esteem and healthy families who need you most. The major and minor figures in these children's lives are already taking care of business. But the other children, whose numbers are increasing, need you desperately. Teachers may not be their last hope, but they are their last easy hope. Therapy can be an arduous journey; jail has been known to turn a life around; gangs offer membership and belonging. I prefer to see a child touched and helped by a teacher. Never underestimate a teacher's impact. Realize it may take years to unfold.

Elizabeth Silance Ballard illustrates this beautifully in "Three Letters from Teddy":

I have not seen Teddy Stallard since he was in my fifth-grade class, fifteen years ago. It was early in my career, and I had only been teaching for two years.

From the first day he stepped into my classroom, I disliked Teddy.... He was dirty. Not just occasionally, but all the time.... He knew I didn't like him, but he didn't know why. Nor did I know - then or now - why I felt such an intense dislike for him. All I know is that he was a little boy no one cared about, and I made no effort in his behalf....

As the Christmas holidays approached, I knew that Teddy would never catch up in time to be promoted to the sixth-grade level. He would be a repeater.

To justify myself, I went to his cumulative folder from time to time. He had very low grades for the first four years, but no grade failure. How had he made it, I didn't know. I closed my mind to the personal remarks:

First grade: "Teddy shows promise by work and attitude, but has poor home situation.

Second grade: "Teddy could do better. Mother terminally ill. He receives little help at home."

Third grade: "Teddy is a pleasant boy. Helpful, but too serious. Slow learner. Mother passed away at the end of the year."

Fourth grade: "Very slow, but well behaved. Father shows no interest."

Well, they passed him four times, but he will certainly repeat fifth grade! Do him good! I said to myself....

Teachers always get several gifts at Christmas, but mine that year seemed bigger and more and more elaborate than ever.... His gift was the last one I picked up.... Its wrapping was a brown paper bag and he had colored Christmas trees and red balls all over it. It was stuck together with masking tape.

The group was completely silent and for the first time I felt conspicuous, embarrassed because they all stood watching me unwrap that gift.

As I removed the last bit of masking tape, two items fell to my desk. A gaudy rhinestone bracelet with several stones missing and a small bottle of dime-store cologne - half empty.

I could hear the snickers and whispers and I wasn't sure I could look at Teddy.

"Isn't this lovely?" I asked, placing the bracelet on my wrist. "Teddy, would you help me fasten it?"

He smiled shyly as he fixed the clasp and I held up my wrist for all of them to admire.

There were a few hesitant *ooh's* and *aah's* but as I dabbed the cologne behind my ears, all the girls lined up for a dab behind their ears....

We ate our refreshments and the bell rang.... When they had all left, he [Teddy] walked towards me....

"You smell just like Mom," he said softly. "Her bracelet looks real pretty on you, too. I'm glad you liked it."

He left quickly and I locked the door, sat down at my desk and wept, resolving to make up to Teddy what I had deliberately deprived him of - a teacher who cared.

Slowly but surely he caught up with the rest of the class. Gradually there was a definite upward curve in his grades.

He did not have to repeat fifth grade. In fact his final averages were among the highest in the class.

I did not hear from Teddy until seven years later, when his first letter appeared in my mailbox.

"Dear Miss Thompson,
I just wanted you to be the first to know. I will be graduating second in my class next month. Very truly yours, Teddy Stallard."

Four years later, Teddy's second letter came.

"Dear Miss Thompson,
I wanted you to be the first to know. I was just informed that I'll be graduating first in my class. The university has not been easy, but I liked it. Very truly yours, Teddy Stallard"

And now - today - Teddy's third letter.

"Dear Miss Thompson,
I wanted you to be the first to know. As of today I am Theodore J. Stallard, MD. How about that!!??

I'm going to be married in July, the twenty-seventh, to be exact. I wanted to ask you if you could come and sit where Mom would sit if she were here. I'll have no family there as Dad died last year. Very truly yours, Ted Stallard"

I'm not sure what kind of gift one sends to a doctor on completion of medical school and state boards. Maybe I'll just wait and take a wedding gift, but my note can't wait.

"Dear Ted,
Congratulations! You made it and you did it yourself! In spite of those like me and not because of us, this day has come for you.

God bless you. I'll be at the wedding with bells on!"

There are thousands of Teddy Stallards all over our nation - the children we have forgotten or given up on.

Each of us knows one. How many will we let slip through our fingers. How many will never become who and what they might have been.

The Sunshine Effect

The Sunshine Effect is a concept I have grappled with for years. Early in my professional career, I worked as a school psychologist, first as an intern where each of us was moved around to numerous schools and school districts, probably to see how we would fare in various environments. In my first early years, I worked with both rural and urban schools in two countries; my work took me to elementary through secondary schools, Kindergarten through grade thirteen, and in both regular and special education programs. From this quick, broad education, and despite my youth, I quickly came to realize how very alike all schools are in some general ways and how extraordinarily different they are in the rest of the components. I also learned that I (or anyone) can determine much about the principal of a school before meeting her by simply walking through her school. The same, it turns out, is true for directors of early childhood programs and for teachers in classrooms and for parents in homes. Each of these pivotal figures sets the tone for the entire school or classroom or home, a vital, discernible atmosphere. Each brings their own *presence* to the setting. There are many nuances to these personally set ambiances, and it is helpful to each of us to be aware that we set a tone around ourselves that affects other people and permeates the environment near us. It is helpful to be aware of what tone we exude.

The tone I'm speaking of here is best likened to sunshine and clouds. Some schools and classrooms, like some homes, are filled with sunshine and light; joy, contentment, and health abound. Still others seem covered by clouds and pervaded with darkness; fear, discontent, and gloom prevail. It seems that in our positions, dynamic positions as educators or parents, we do set the tone on a daily basis for those around us. Have you ever noticed that when you are tired, irritable, or stressful, the children have a terrible day; if it can go wrong, it does go wrong. By contrast, when you are loaded with energy and good will, and ready to handle anything, little happens.

We radiate who we are and what we feel every day. Sometimes I wish I could just once have an off day and not have everything and everyone else seem to fall apart with me. (As the children get older, this wish is coming true.) When we are dealing with young children, this is unlikely. Children pick up on the mood we are in and the tone we set. Over time, they begin to know what to expect, what the feeling usually is around us. How is your tone? Do you generally offer sunshine or clouds? It is this "generally" and "over time" which are important; isolated, infrequent tones are much less significant. What we too often overlook is that we, too, are caught up in the light or the darkness and taken up or down with it. It is difficult to override our own attitude, although this can be accomplished occasionally. Thus, the real question to ask ourselves is: are we most typically filled with sunshine or with darkness. For what we are will out. What we sow, we shall reap.

> Those who bring sunshine into the lives of others cannot keep it from themselves. - J.M. Barrie

You Cannot Give What You Do Not Have

It is true: you cannot give what you do not have. If you have no sunshine within, you will not be able to sustain a sunny atmosphere. More acutely, if you do not have self-esteem established in all three areas, Existence, Accomplishment, and Mistakes, everything previous will become technique only. Not only will these skills fall into disuse, but when used, they will have a false or feigned ring to them. In order to handle mistakes as an opportunity for learning, one must *believe* the concept is true. To be able to convince a child that she has incredible value because she exists, one must *believe* it - not just for the child but for one's own self.

It is absolutely critical that we find ways to build our own self-esteem and make sure that we keep a steady, high balance in our own emotional bank accounts. Faking it is categorically different from *being* it. Solid, high self-esteem is required to work with children.

Create the Best Place to BE

The Best Place to *BE!* Please note first that the phrase is the best place to *BE* not *DO*. Inherent in this concept is that Existence, being not doing, is the foundation of self-esteem. Further, we need to determine whether the home, the family place that we have created, is a good place to be. When your children return home, do their shoulders relax or tense? Are they emotionally comfortable and safe here? Is this a place where they thrive or wither? Do they live in the comfortable knowledge that they are welcome and valued, or live in apprehension that anything may happen and that they really do not belong here? How about you? Do you breathe a sigh of relief when you finally get to the door or do you tense up waiting for the next unpleasant remark or incident? Is this the best place to be, a haven in the stormy seas of the real world? A place where you find solace and people who are glad to see you? If our children do not thrive and feel secure at home, where will they find their worth, their membership, their peace?

For you teachers, fortunately or unfortunately, school is the second most influential place. It is certainly preferable that school is number two; home has the stronger effect on our children. Presently, for increasing numbers of students, home is not a good place to be, let alone the best. Our job, then, is to create a similar type of family and safety within our classrooms; for many of our students, it will be the best place to be. Too often children reach adolescence never having had a good place to be, no emotional safety, no warm, welcome place of membership. These children are vulnerable to gangs and drugs. It is, therefore, critical that when you walk into your classroom each morning (well, nine days out of ten) that you are entering the (second) Best Place to *BE* for you - certainly the Best Place to Work.

One of my favorite teachers, perhaps the most affirming teacher either of my children had, inadvertently gave me the secret to being a genuinely affirming teacher, or person for that matter. For months I had asked her what the secret to her magic was, and she had given me various tips for building self-esteem. I kept thinking that each was a nice technique, but it was not what I wanted to know. What I wanted was the *key* to her magic. Then one year I had lunch with her at a teacher professional development program the day before school started. She was happy to be going back into the classroom and excited about meeting her new students and starting a brand new year. Most teachers are. But, the sentences this teacher used gave away the secret: "I don't know what I would do if they didn't let me teach. I love teaching. I am a teacher." Teaching is not just what she does; *it is who she is.* Second only to her home, her classroom is the best place for her to be, and, consequently, a best place for her students to be.

Navigating the Tunnels

Funerals are always difficult to attend; funerals where a suicide has occurred are even more so. Sadly, the last two funerals I have attended were for men who had taken their own lives. Earlier, we considered one of these incidents; now we will address one aspect of the second. Each of us has had to wrestle with discouragement in our lives. Perhaps it is more accurate to say we have been oppressed by it. We seem to lose the will to continue when we become discouraged. Not wanting to wrestle any longer, or becoming paralyzed, becomes the core problem. We need to understand and come to believe firmly in the lessons of Navigating the Tunnels. These lessons provide immunization against suicide.

Everyone's life will contain problems or, shall we say, tunnels. This is a given. The first lesson we encounter teaches: **Expect problems. Life is a journey filled with both open road and tunnels.** When we realize that problems befall everyone, we can avoid becoming terribly upset when they do occur.

Since our road will have some tunnels, we will require bright, functioning headlights. Or, in other words, we will need procedures or skills to help us maneuver through the tunnels, the times of darkness. The second lesson is that we will each need to develop beneficial and productive problem-solving skills to deal with our problems. As we develop these skills, we begin to learn the second lesson, which is: **Tunnels can be navigated; problems can be solved.**

The last lesson takes place at the end of the tunnel: **There is light at the end of every tunnel. Don't give up hope.** Of course, I could be wrong, and we will never have proof, but I am quite certain that everyone who chooses suicide as a permanent answer to a temporary problem has lost this lesson. This last lesson clearly reflects the third Critical Life Message, "There is no problem so great I cannot deal with it."

These tunnel lessons are some of the most crucial lessons we can ever teach and learn. One of the most important tasks we will ever undertake is to engender and fortify these three lessons in our children. These lessons ought to be 'required immunization' for all.

Frogkissing

Whenever I present ideas on self-esteem to early childhood educators and teachers, I include a segment which speaks to one aspect of their job descriptions which is ofttimes overlooked. (Mothers or fathers may also enjoy this approach.) The next time you find yourself at a boring cocktail party, your spouse's office Christmas party, or anywhere where someone asks you what you do with that "justify your existence" twist to it, try telling them you are a *Frogkisser*. I concede this is assuredly taking the low road, but sometimes taking the low road is more fun. (And most of us do not have enough fun in our lives.) For in truth, kissing frogs, just like in the fairy tale, is exactly what you do.

In many ways it is largely frogs, with many lessons to learn, who come hopping through our doors each day. Yet within each one is hidden a prince (or princess). It is our job to kiss these froggies and help them turn into princes. The fable was right on two accounts; it misled us on one. First, we must never forget that children come to us essentially as uncivilized little bozos, and I mean this in the most affectionate and kindest way. They have so much to learn about themselves and the world (the uncivilized part), and they are carefree, free spirits (the bozo part). Both of these attributes are as they should and must be. This is why I so easily picture any child as a little frog with a prince hiding and waiting inside. We must be able to see not just what they are, but what they can and will be. Thus, the first truth in the fable is that within each frog-child is a prince awaiting awakening and freedom.

The second point which the fable makes is that it takes a princess or prince, royalty not ordinary folk, or at least someone very gifted and with a very special touch, to release the prince inside the frog. Virtually anyone can make a chair. But it takes a *skilled and gifted* woodworker, who has a keen understanding of wood and chairs, to find and release an exquisite chair from the wood. Anyone can work with, care for, and teach frog-children. But it takes a *skilled and gifted and caring* teacher or parent, who understands children and grown-ups, to find and release the prince within a child. The difference between the woodworker and the parent or teacher is that we can afford to bungle the chair; we get another chunk of wood and try again. We cannot afford to bungle any child. *No child is replaceable.*

If you bungle raising your children, I don't think whatever else you do well matters very much. - Jacqueline Kennedy Onassis

We certainly do get to make mistakes along the way. It is not the inevitable mishandlings or miswordings from which a child cannot recover. It is a parent or teacher continually on the wrong path, with weak skills and vision, who in the end has bungled and hurt a child. It is one thing to make mistakes and follow up with damage control and learning. It is another thing entirely to continually remake the same type of mistake and to even escalate mistakes and hurt and warp a child.

It is critical that caregivers and teachers be well-trained and gifted *professionals*. As well, it is crucial that parents become well-trained and skilled parents. Anything less, places at risk our most precious gifts, our most significant assets, and our future. We owe it to our children to have a fair idea of what we are doing and where we are headed. Training manuals do not come with children, but training manuals are available for those who are interested and willing to take precious time to search them out. You will need one, for as Bette Davis said in All About Eve, "it *is* going to be a bumpy night." Rearing children is bumpy business.

There is no more difficult and meaningful job than bringing up children. Time, thought, and effort will be required.

The element of the Frog and Princess fable that is misleading comes near the end of the story. Here, the princess finally kisses the frog, and lo and behold, he instantly, straightaway turns into the prince. I don't think so. Not in real life. In reality, we must kiss each of our frogs thousands of times over months and years to free the whole prince. Countless affirming skills and interactions are needed. Start kissing. To be an affirming parent or teacher, one has to acquire a taste for frog and a gift for magic!

These moments of frog-kissing become touchstones throughout the child's life. In the past he was someone valuable and important to himself and to someone else. A child can, and will, return to these touchstones in times of doubt and discouragement (frogginess). In this way his value *cannot ever* be taken away.

PART V - THE JOURNEY CONTINUES

Process

Parenting, and working with children, is an ongoing process. We learn; we practice; we succeed; we fail; we try again. What is important is that we *strive* to be the best parent for our child(ren) that we can possibly be. Remember the monkey in the side car. We do not have to get it right moment by moment and in every instance; we just need to get it mostly right and get our children going in the right general direction. We just need to take action, based on thinking and planning and ever increasing vision and wisdom. There is no crime in making mistakes or we would all be in prison! The crimes, if you will, are in not learning from mistakes and not recognizing the far-reaching import of your assignment as parent. How you choose to discipline, how you choose to communicate, what principles and life lessons you choose to teach, what life messages you choose to send, these signify who *you* are.

Guilt

It is my mission to reduce guilt among parents, not increase it. As well, I strive to increase integrity and confidence. Vision (recognizing where you want to end up) and skills (finding ways to get there) increase confidence and permit integrity. Consequently guilt and anguish diminish. It is a myth that raising children is a dreadful, thankless task which goes from bad to worse when children reach adolescence. The greatest joys in my life have happened because of my children and husband. And I am not alone in this feeling. Having children has caused me to develop character and traits (mostly positive) which I would never have had without having been a parent. I would not trade the experience of being a mother to my sons for anything in the world. I wish I had known this truth when they were young and I was so lost; this knowledge would have been most comforting. If you invest in your skills and wisdom while your children are young, though it is never too late, then during your children's rocky teen years, you will reap what you have sown. For these years are indeed the toughest on the children. Would you go back to age thirteen? I wouldn't, not for a moment! One of my greatest sources of strength is a growing, quiet confidence I have about my children. They are becoming less frog and more prince every day!

Please do not let what you have learned here or in any book make you feel guilty about the past. Instead, when you catch yourself doing something you recognize as unhelpful, pat yourself on the back for knowing more today than yesterday. And offer yourself understanding - change takes time, is frustrating, and can be awfully stressful. If parenting were easy and natural, none of us would struggle. Trust me, everyone is challenged by being a parent. Everyone.

Tolerance

Tolerance is a virtue, and one seen less and less frequently. It is important to develop tolerance for other parents and other teachers. It is exceedingly important that you develop this for the other parent(s) of your children, birth and step. No one agrees entirely on an issue as complicated as parenting. I will turn to the Bible (John 8:7) for words of wisdom, "He that is without sin among you, let him first cast a stone...." No one has all the answers. Many answers work. Each of us finds answers in our own time. Teaching, not criticizing, hastens answers.

Tolerance for our children's differences from us (and there will be many - it is their job to separate from us) will also be important; with our teens, it is required. Your children are not you. Their job is to discover who they are. They must make their own mistakes. No one can live his life for or as someone else.

Gifts

There are only two lasting gifts we give our children, however clichéd this sounds: one is roots, the other, wings. Most of us invest so much time, effort, and thought into helping our children become grounded and rooted and secure, that when it comes time to soar, we adults hang on for dear life. Some of us are afraid that this soaring can lead to crashing to the ground. To be comfortable with themselves and secure in their own worth and identity, children need roots. But to be confident and courageous and free, to be *herself or himself,* every child will need wings. Please do not stop at roots. Freedom is essential and the fun part. It takes wings to enter adulthood. Isn't that where we were headed from the outset?

> You are the bows from which your children as living arrows
> are sent forth. - Kahlil Gibran, *The Prophet*

And lastly, I ask you to take this, as my husband would say, as seriously as a heart attack. Nothing is more important or meaningful than bringing up emotionally whole and healthy, happy children. My husband also understands the importance and wisdom of fun. It is not going to be worth it if you cannot manage to find the fun and enjoyment in family life. You will choose to leave your family or perhaps worse, resent and begrudge your time spent in it. Thus, I also implore you to recognize (almost constantly and even in the worst moments) that your children are the most precious gifts you will ever receive. Although it may seem entirely out of the realm of possibility, they do grow up and leave, probably much, much sooner than you would ever believe. And you will miss them. Will they want to return on occasion? That's entirely up to you. Thus, I entreat you to enjoy them simply as much, and as often, as you can. For truly, they are life's most precious gift.

Notes

Part I

1   Dodd testimony to U.S. Congressional Joint Session hearing on Keeping Every Child Safe, March 10, 1993.

2   Edelman testimony to U.S. Congressional Joint Session hearing on Keeping Every Child Safe, March 10, 1993.

3   "Day Care & Early Education," 1991.

4   For additional information concerning allowances and chores, you may find Barbara Coloroso's audio tape, "Winning at Parenting Without Beating Your Kids" helpful.

Part II

5   See text by Faber and Mazlish, *How to Talk So Kids Will Listen & Listen So Kids Will Talk*. New York: Avon Books, 1980. I am indebted to these authors for their concept of barriers to cooperation and descriptive language.

6   See text by M.H. Popkin, *Active Parenting*. Atlanta: Active Parenting, Inc., 1983.

Part III

7   See text by Dreikurs and Grey, *A New Approach to Discipline: Logical Consequences*. New York: Hawthorn Books, Inc., 1968. I am indebted to these authors for their concept of logical consequences upon which Disciplinary Consequences is based.

8   I am indebted to Barbara Coloroso for the technique of mutual permission.

9   See text by Thomas Gordon, *Teaching Children Self-Discipline*. New York: Random House, 1989. The title of this text was later changed to *Discipline That Works*. I am indebted to Dr. Gordon for these three strategies and the transition phrases.

Part IV

10 Clarke, J.I., *Self-Esteem: A Family Affair*. San Francisco, CA: Harper & Rowe, 1981. I am indebted to Mrs. Clarke for the concepts of Being, Doing, and Can Do Better upon which the concepts Existence, Accomplishment, and Mistakes are based.

11 These audio and video programs are available from Stairway Education Programs. Call 1-817-488-4664 or 1-800-422-4337 for additional information.

12 Ginott, H.G., *Between Parent and Child*. New York: Avon Books, 1956.

13 "Day Care & Early Education" 1991.

14 TAEYC, 1993.

15 See text by Faber & Mazlish, *Liberated Parents Liberated Children*. New York: Avon Books, 1974, p.65.

16 Grant, L.T., "Harper's" October 1979. I am indebted to Mrs. Curran for directing me to this particular article.

References

Andrews, R. *The Columbia Dictionary of Quotations*. New York: Columbia University Press.

Aspy and Roebuck. *Kids Don't Learn From People They Don't Like*. Amherst, MA: Human Resource Development Press, 1977.

Ballard, E.S. "Three Letters from Teddy" *Home Life*, March 1976. ©1976 The Sunday School Board of the Southern Baptist Convention. All rights reserved. Used by permission of the author.

Bartlett's Familiar Quotations. Boston, MA: Little, Brown and Company.

Briggs, D.C. *Celebrate Yourself*. Garden City, NY: Doubleday & Company, Inc., 1977.

Briggs, D.C. *Your Child's Self-Esteem: The Key to Life*. Garden City, NY: Doubleday & Company, Inc., 1970.

Cansler, Martin, and Valand. *Working with Families*. Chapel Hill, NC: Kaplan Press, 1976.

"CDF Reports" February, 1994, Vol 15, No 3. Washington, DC: CDF, 1994.

Clark, J.I. *Self-Esteem: A Family Affair*. San Francisco, CA: Harper & Row, 1981.

Clark, J.I. and Dawson, C. *Growing Up Again: Parenting Ourselves, Parenting Our Children*. New York: Harper & Row, 1989.

Coloroso, B. *Discipline: Winning at Teaching*. Boulder, CO: kids are worth it, inc., 1987.

Coopersmith, S. *The Antecedents of Self-Esteem*. San Francisco, CA: W.H. Freeman & Co., 1967.

Covey, S. *Principle-Centered Leadership*. New York: Summit Books, Simon & Schuster, 1990.

Covey, S. *The Seven Habits of Highly Effective People*. New York: Simon & Schuster, 1990.

Curran, D. *Traits of A Healthy Family*. New York: HarperCollins Publishers, 1983.

Curwin, R. and Mendler, A. *Discipline With Dignity*. Alexandria, VA: Association for Supervision and Curriculum Development, 1988.

Dreikurs and Grey. *A New Approach to Discipline: Logical Consequences*. New York: Hawthorn Books, Inc., 1968.

Faber, A. and Mazlish, E. *How To Talk So Kids Will Listen & Listen So Kids Will Talk*. New York: Avon Books, 1980.

Faber, A. and Mazlish, E. *Liberated Parents Liberated Children*. New York: Avon Books, 1974.

Fisher, R. and Ury, W. *Getting to Yes: Negotiating Agreement Without Giving In*. Boston: Houghton Mifflin Company, 1981. New York: Penguin Books, 1983.

Ginott, H.G., *Between Parent and Child*. New York: Avon Books, 1956.

Gordon, T. *P.E.T. Parent Effectiveness Training*. New York: Peter H. Wyden, Inc., 1970.

Gordon, T. *Teaching Children Self-Discipline*. New York: Random House, 1989. The title of this text was later changed to *Discipline That Works*.

Greven, P. *Spare the Child: The Religious Roots of Punishment and the Psychological Impact of Physical Abuse*. New York: Alfred A. Knopf, Inc., 1991. New York: Vintage Books, Inc., 1992.

Kohn, A. *No Contest: The Case Against Competition*. Boston: Houghton Mifflin Company, 1986.

Lombardi, D. and Corsini, R. *C4R: A New System of Schooling*. Holistic Education, 1988.

Popkin, M.H. *Active Parenting Handbook*. Atlanta: Active Parenting, Inc., 1983.

Satir, V., *Peoplemaking*. Palo Alto, CA: Science and Behavior Books, Inc., 1972.

The Rubicon Dictionary of Positive, Motivational, Life-Affirming and Inspirational Quotations. Newington, CT: Rubicon Press, 1994.

Webster's Seventh New Collegiate Dictionary. Springfield, MA: G.C. Merriam Company, 1983 ed.

Ziglar, Z. *Raising Positive Kids in a Negative World*. Nashville, TN: Oliver-Nelson Books, 1985.